SpringerBriefs in Computer Science

Series Editors
Stan Zdonik
Peng Ning
Shashi Shekhar
Jonathan Katz
Xindong Wu
Lakhmi C. Jain
David Padua
Xuemin Shen
Borko Furht
V.S. Subrahmanian
Martial Hebert
Katsushi Ikeuchi
Bruno Siciliano

For further volumes:
http://www.springer.com/series/10028

Shui Yu

Distributed Denial of Service Attack and Defense

 Springer

Shui Yu
School of Information Theory
Deakin University
Melbourne, VIC
Australia

ISSN 2191-5768   ISSN 2191-5776 (electronic)
ISBN 978-1-4614-9490-4   ISBN 978-1-4614-9491-1 (eBook)
DOI 10.1007/978-1-4614-9491-1
Springer New York Heidelberg Dordrecht London

Library of Congress Control Number: 2013952909

Printed on acid-free paper

Springer is part of Springer Science+Business Media (www.springer.com)

To Su and Ian

Preface

Since human beings stepped into the Internet era, our lives are deeply involved with the Internet. Many killer applications are carried out through Internet-based applications. At the same time, motivated by huge financial, political, or other rewards, hackers are exhausting their energy to execute cybercrimes. Due to the nature of the Internet and the lack of cyber laws, cyberspace has been a heaven for intelligent attackers. It is easy to launch attacks, but hard to identify the persons who commit the attacks. It is even harder to bring them to justice.

To date, one critical attack in cyberspace is the distributed denial-of-service (DDoS) attack. My study on cybersecurity started in 2007. I am attracted by this topic not only because of the problem itself but also the bigger research field of cyberspace. It is generally agreed that the current Internet research lacks theoretical foundation. Research indicates that our understanding of the cyberspace is limited and there are a huge unexplored territory in cyberspace for both academical and industrial participants.

This book brief is mainly based on our research of the DDoS problem. For readers' convenience, we try to make each chapter relatively independent. Moreover, we pay a special attention on methodology and mathematical modelling and expect to benefit readers for their potential research in related fields. Constrained by my knowledge and capability, the content of this book brief is very shallow in terms of mathematical modelling. However, I decide not to hide my disadvantage in order to save a bit time for some beginners who may work on the related fields.

I would like to thank the editor of this series, Professor Sherman Shen, for his constructive guidance and kind help. Thanks are also noted for the team of Springer for their patience and assistance.

I also would like to take this opportunity to thank Professor Yue Wu, Professor Yi Zhang, and Professor Wanlei Zhou for bringing me to the academic world. During these years study on DDoS, my colleagues, co-authors, and many people offered me their guidance, support, and help, such as Professor Ivan Stojmenovic, Professor Kai Hwang, and Mr Bin Liu. The list is too long to complete here, but I do appreciate their time and effort from the bottom of my heart. I especially thank Professor Weijia Jia from City University of Hong Kong, Professor Weifa Liang from Australia

National University, and Professor Song Guo from University of Aizu and their institutions for the financial support of my visits. I am grateful to Professor Yong Xiang and Dr Simon James for their continuous discussion and help on research and paper writing.

In particular, I would like to thank my wife, Su, for her understanding and full support for my research.

Melbourne, Australia   Dr Shui Yu

Contents

Chapter 1
An Overview of DDoS Attacks

Abstract In this chapter, we firstly review the short history of denial of service (DoS) and distributed denial of service (DDoS) attacks. We further explore the reasons why the current cyberspace is a heaven for cyber criminals, such as DDoS attackers. We present the challenges of the DDoS related research fields from various aspects, and discuss the possible research methods and strategies to serve the challenges.

1.1 Introduction

The Internet has become an important part of our society in numerous ways, such as in economics, government, business, and daily personal life. Further, an increasing amount of critical infrastructures, e.g., power grid, air traffic control, are managed and controlled via the Internet, in addition to traditional infrastructure for communication. However, today's cyberspace is full of attacks, such as Distributed Denial of Service (DDoS), information phishing, financial fraud, email spamming, and so on.

We can see that cyberspace has become a heaven for intelligent criminals, who are motivated by significant financial or political reward. According to an annual report from the FBI's Internet Crime Complaint Centre, financial loss resulting from cyber attack totalled US$559.7 million in 2009. Symantec identified more than 5.5 billion malicious attacks in 2011, an increase of 81 % over the previous year. Moreover, the number of unique malware variants increased to 403 million, and the number of web attacks per day increased by 36 %.

Among various Internet based attacks, Denial of Service (DoS) attack is a critical and continuous threat in cyber security. In general, DoS attacks are implemented by either forcing a victim computer to reset, or consuming its resources, e.g., CPU cycles, memory or network bandwidth. As a result, the targeted computer can no longer provide its intended services to its legitimate users. When the DoS attacks are organized by multiple distributed computers, it is called distributed denial of

S. Yu, *Distributed Denial of Service Attack and Defense*, SpringerBriefs in Computer
Science, DOI 10.1007/978-1-4614-9491-1_1, © The Author(s) 2014

service attack, which is a popular attack method in the cyberspace. From classical textbooks, we know security falls into three categories: confidentiality, availability and integrity. It is obvious that DDoS attacks belong to the availability category.

The idea of denial of service has been in place for a long time in human history, such as city besiegment in ancient wars. This concept firstly appeared in the digital world in 1984 from the research on operating systems [1]. With the booming of the Internet in the middle of the 1990s, DDoS attacks are getting more and more familiar to general public. There are numerous survey papers on DDoS attacks from various perspectives, such as [2] and [3].

It is reported that there were only six DDoS related attacks in 1988, and the number of attacks has been increasing in an exponential style. At the same time, attack rates continuously reached high levels. In year 2000, well-known web sites, such as CNN, Amazon and Yahoo, became the targets of DDoS attacks, and the attack rate was around 1 GB per second. A report showed that a DDoS attack rate reached 70 GB per second in 2007. As we are writing this book, many Internet users have experienced the "biggest DDoS attack" in history in March 2013. The peak of the attack reached 300 GB per second. We truly believe this record will be beaten again in the near future, believe it or not.

The purpose of early attacks was mainly for fun and curiosity about technology. However, we have recently witnessed an explosive increase in cyber attacks due to the huge financial or political rewards for cyber attackers. The news of DDoS attacks occupies the headlines of newspapers from time to time. It is not surprise that many nations have established their cyber armies. For example, on June 19, 2012, the Washington Post reported that the US and Israel governments launched two sophisticated viruses, Flame and Stuxnet, in order to disrupt Iran's petroleum production and distribution infrastructure and its uranium-enrichment facilities.

Despite all the efforts from industry participants and academia, DDoS attack is still an open problem, and there are many challenges that we have to overcome. For example, we are embarrassed to face inquiries from the public, such as who are cyber criminals? and where are they? We list some of the essential reasons for this passive situation as follows.

1. The no security design of the ARPARNET network. As we know, the Internet came from the private network, ARPARNET. As a private network, there were very limited security concerns in the original design. However, the private network became a public network in the 1990s, and now many killer applications are running on the Internet, such as e-business. Many security patches have been developed and installed to circumvent the inherent vulnerabilities, however, the effectiveness of these efforts are sometimes limited. For example, the Internet was designed in a stateless style, therefore, a receiver has no information about which routers a received packet went through. Moreover, it is easy to perform source IP spoofing.

2. The Internet is the largest man-made system in human history. The cyberspace is huge and complex, and stays in an anarchy status. It is impossible to force a policy to all parties of the Internet, and collaboration among different ISPs

is hard to implement security policies. More importantly, there are ISPs who support malicious activities for financial or political purposes.

3. Cyber attackers are enjoying one incredible advantage of the cyberspace: it is hard for defenders to technically identify attackers. Moreover, there lacks international laws or agreements among nations to bring cyber criminals to justice who commit crimes in one country but are living in other countries.

4. Hacking tools and software are easy to obtained. As a result, an attacker may not need profound knowledge of networking or operating system to initiate a cyber attack.

1.2 How to Launch DDoS Attacks

In general, DDoS attacks can be launched in two forms. The first one targets to crash a system by sending one or more carefully crafted packets, which are designed based the vulnerability of the victim. For example, the "ping-of-death" attack, which can cause some operating systems to crash, freeze, or reboot. This form of DDoS can be defeated by patching the system vulnerabilities. The second form DDoS is to use a large amount of traffic to exhaust the resources of a victim, such as network bandwidth, computing power, operating system data structures, and so on. As a result, the quality of service of the victim is significantly degraded or disabled to its legitimate clients. Compared with the first form, the second form of DDoS attack is hard to deal with. In the rest of this book, we focus this kind of DDoS attack.

In order to launch an effective DDoS attack, cyber attackers have to firstly establish a network of computers, which is known as a *botnet* or *army*. We call the people who control a botnet as *botmasters* or *botnet owners*.

In order to organize a botnet, attackers take advantage of various methods to find vulnerable hosts on the Internet to gain access to them. Attackers generally use different kinds of techniques (referred to as *scanning techniques*) to find vulnerable machines [4]. The next step for the attacker is to install programs (known as *attack tools*) on the compromised hosts. The hosts running these attack tools are known as *bots* or *zombies* [2, 5, 6]. The headquarter of a botnet is call *command and control (C&C)* server. It is necessary for a *C&C* server to communicate with its bots for a number of reasons, such as updating the attack tools, and issuing an attack order.

In order to sustain their *C&C* servers from detection, botnet programmers may set up a few intermediate nodes as step stones between the *C&C* server and bots. They also take cryptography techniques to encrypt the messages of their communication. Moreover, in order to avoid evictions, botnet programmers are taking various techniques, such as IP flux or domain flux, to sustain their *C&C* servers. Consequently, they also need to design novel strategies for their bots to phone home.

There are two different DDoS attack classes: typical DDoS attack and DRDoS (Distributed Reflection Denial of Service) attack. The hosts of both categories are

Fig. 1.1 A typical distributed
denial of service attack

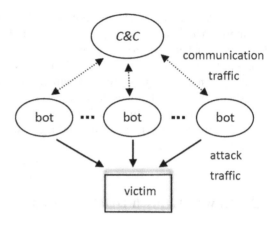

compromised machines that have been recruited during the scanning process and
are installed with malicious code.

As shown in Fig. 1.1, in a typical DDoS attack, an attacker coordinates and orders
the *C&C* server, and in turn, it coordinates and triggers bots. More specifically, the
attacker sends an attack command to the *C&C* server who activates all attack processes on the bots, which are in hibernation, waiting for the appropriate command
to wake up and start attacking. Then, *C&C* servers, through these processes, send
attack commands to bots, ordering them to mount a DDoS attack against a victim.
By doing it this way, the bots begin to send a large volume of packets to the victim,
flooding its system with useless load and exhausting its resources.

Unlike a typical DDoS attacks, a DRDoS attack network consists of *C&C* servers
and reflectors as shown in Fig. 1.2. The scenario of this type of attack is the same as
that of a typical DDoS attack up to a specific stage. The attackers have control over
C&C servers, which, in turn, have control over bots. The difference with a DRDoS
attack is that bots, led by *C&C* servers, send a stream of packets with the victim's IP
address as the source IP address to other uninfected machines (known as *reflectors*).
This exhorts these innocent machines to connect to the victim because they believe
that the victim was the host that requested it. As a result, there is a large amount of
traffic to the victim from the reflectors for the opening of a new connections.

Researchers from academia and industry have proposed a number of methods
to defend against the DDoS threat. Despite these efforts, DDoS attacks still remain
a huge threat. Attackers manage to explore new weaknesses in computer systems
and communication protocols after known weaknesses have been patched up. In
some cases, attackers also exploit defense mechanisms in order to develop attacks
to conquer these mechanisms or exploit them to generate false alarms and cause
catastrophic results.

In general, DDoS defence can be classified into three categories: detection,
mitigation and traceback. We will explore these three aspects in the rest of this
book.

Fig. 1.2 A distributed
reflection denial of service
attack

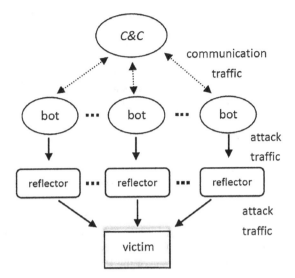

As we know the ICT world develops quickly, and we witness new applications from time to time. Whenever there is a new computing platform or new computing model, cyber criminals will quickly develop their tools and weapons to commit their malicious tasks.

With the booming of cloud computing, cyber attackers have targeted on this new computing platform. We have seen reports on DDoS attacks in clouds. A variation of a DDoS attack in cloud computing is the Economic Denial of Sustainability (EDoS) attack [7] or the Fraudulent Resource Consumption (FRC) attack [8]. There are also many researches have been done in this field. For example, Lua and Yow [9] proposed to establish a large swarm network to mitigate DDoS attack on cloud, and an intelligent fast-flux technique is used to balance the work load. However, we truly believe that there are many new questions to be answered in this battle ground. We list some of the interesting questions as follows.

1. Can a super DDoS attack disable the service of a cloud data center?
2. How should we deal with DDoS attacks on cloud hosted services?
3. How can we prevent malicious parties to rent cloud resources to mount DDoS attacks?
4. What should a cloud firewall look like?

1.3 Challenges in DDoS Related Research

As we have seen in the previous sections, defenders are quite passive and vulnerable against DDoS attacks due to the no-security original design, complexity and super large scale of the Internet, and the anarchy management fashion. We cannot change these factors as they are already in place. We are more interested in how to address problems. In our understanding, we can address the problem in threefold as follows.

1. Understand the cyberspace theoretically and deeply. Due the the fact that we have a very limited understanding of the cyberspace, the American National Research Council proposed a new research field as *network science* in 2006, and targeting to advance our knowledge of networks and networking [10]. The Internet is a major study object of the network science. Moreover, the majority of current dominant Internet modeling is based on the random graph model proposed in 1959 [11], which is far before the birth date of the Internet and the Web; More and more recent observations indicate that there is a great discrepancy between the random graph based models and the reality. Started around the end of last century, new discoveries and models of the Internet and the Web were reported constantly, such as the small world model [12], the scale free model [13], and the complex networks [14]. Power law (which is usually represented by the Zipf distribution or the Pareto distribution) was found pervasive in nature, economics and man-made systems, such as individual income among a group of people, word frequency in a language. Scientists have also found many power law phenomenon in the cyberspace. For example, the popularity of web pages follows the Zipf distribution [15], the size of web documents follows the Pareto distribution [16]. Is power law pervasive or dominant in the cyber space? Researchers cannot answer this question so far. Moreover, IEEE is launching a new journal, IEEE Transactions on Network Science and Engineering, which is focusing on network science.
2. Understand our cyber opponents in a correct way. Due to security and privacy reasons, it is hard for us to collect or share cyber attack data from industry participants and government agencies. As a result, we can only image our cyber opponent with partial or even misleading information. In order to win the battle, we have to understand our opponents in time and in a correct way.
3. Design and implement effective and efficient strategies to beat cyber crimes. With the solid output of the previous two aspects, we can make effective strategies to beat cyber attacks, including DDoS attacks. However, this step looks a bit far from today as we are struggling at the first and second steps.

We therefore discuss the three aspects in detail in the rest of this chapter for interested readers in the unfolding battle against cyber crimes.

1.3.1 Malicious Networks

Botnet has become the engine of cyber attacks, and it is a typical and dominant malicious network. In this section, we present a summary on what have been done by the research community in this field, more detailed information about botnet will be discussed in Chap. 2.

A botnet is a group of compromised computers on the Internet, and is controlled by botmasters through control and command centres (also referred as to *CC*). Examples of botnets include DSNXbot, evilbot, G-Sysbot, sdbot, and Spybot [5,17]. Botnets are the major attack networks behind various attacks in current cyberspace. Botnets are pervasive, existing simultaneously in many commercial, production and control networks. The size of a botnet could be as large as millions [18]. Because of a large number of machines, botnets can be lethal in bringing down targeted networks, either power grids or air traffic control networks, or communication networks.

On top of the complex of structure and dynamics of the cyberspace, botnet owners are exhausting their energy to disguise botnet activities and traces against detection and elimination. Attackers have at their disposal state-of-the-art techniques, such as stepping stone, reflector, IP spoofing [2, 3], code obfuscation, memory encryption [19], and peer-to-peer implementation technology [3, 17] to cover and sustain their bots. One critical issue for botnet writers is making sure that all bots can contact their CC centre while the physical server and IP of CC centres are kept changing frequently in order to avoid detection or elimination. One common practice by botmasters is "IP fast-fluxing", where the botnet owner constantly keeps changing the IP-addresses mapped to a CC server [20]. The shortcoming for this method is that the botnet is easy to be destroyed once the domain name is known to defenders. In order to overcome this disadvantage, botnet writers, such as Conficker, Kraken and Torpig, have recently developed a new method: "domain fluxing" [5], where each bot algorithmically generates a large set of domain names and queries each of them until one of them is resolved, and then the bot contacts the corresponding IP-address obtained that is typically used to host the command-and-control server [21]. In case of a combination of the two happens, this would be even more difficult to detect. The current method against domain fluxing is to catch bots using honeypots, and use reverse engineering to obtain the URL generation algorithm, which is time consuming and of low accuracy. It is hard to detect bots as the infected computers continuously functioning as normal machines. Besides the techniques that hackers are using, the duration of botnet activities is usually short and random to defenders, which makes it tougher for defenders to collect botnet related data.

Botnet has been investigated from various angles for around 10 years. McGrath and Gupta analysed botnet characteristics, such as IP address distribution, who is records and lexical features of phishing and non-phishing URLs [22]. Researchers employ statistical learning techniques based on lexical features (length of domain names, host names, number of dots in the URL etc.) and other features of URLs to automatically determine if a URL is malicious, i.e., used for phishing or advertising spam [23]. Perdisci et al. implemented a detection mechanism based on passive DNS traffic analysis against IP fast fluxing [20]. Xie et al. focused on detecting spamming botnets by developing regular expression based signatures from a data set of spam URLs [24]. Recently, special techniques have been developed for detecting botnets. It is expected that infiltrated or subverted machines (acting as bots) will contact the botmaster at regular time intervals and these contact times can yield an opportunity for their detection [5, 18]. Bothunter [25], botminer [26] are two such tools employing these techniques. Network telescopes have been employed to observe malicious traffic at various vantage points of networks [27].

The above covers the majority of the work from cyber security community. As we just discussed, we can see that our understanding of botnets or malicious networks is shallow, and many questions remain to be answered.

1.3.2 Data Collection of Malicious Networks

For privacy and security reasons, it is hard to collect attack data from ISPs and related companies. The available data set are usually collected by honeypots [28], glob experimental networks, such as the planet lab [29], or large scale monitoring systems [30,31]. The problem is that usually the data are not the ones that we expect exactly. For instance, the observation range is not what we desire, some information are missing, e.g. routes. Due to this fact, we desperately need mathematical tools to infer a complete picture of malicious network using the partial information that we have, such as the recently invented tool of compressed sensing [32]. There are plenty work to do to fit the related mathematical tools to address this problem that we face.

Even with expected data is in place, we still face a challenge of data processing. It is sure that the data we collected are the mixture of numerous malicious networks. For example, a DNS request failure data set that we obtain is usually the results of multiple botnets. A study of a mixed data set will mislead us with a high probability. In order to study the features of an individual malicious network, we have to separate the mixed data into clusters. We have conducted a preliminary study at a campus network in 2011, which indicated that the bots in the campus network belong to different botnets, and usually one computer may host bots of multiple botnets.

The challenge here is that we do not know how many botnets are there in a collected data set. Previous study on cyber security indicates that bot behaviour among one botnet usually possesses high similarity compared with the bot behavior of other botnets [33, 34]. The similarity could be identified in temporal, spatial or other features. The similarity among a botnet may different from another botnet, and it is not a easy job to identify the similarity of a given botnet.

The unsupervised machine learning is an existing and promising tool for the clustering challenge. The approaches of unsupervised learning include two categories: clustering and blind signal separation. Researchers have proposed many algorithms for this research field, such as principal component analysis, singular value decomposition, mixture models, k-means, and hierarchical clustering [35].

Besides these traditional methods, we also noticed a recently developed technique, graph spectrum [36], which is also promising to address the challenge. Researchers have found that bots from one botnet have more connections, e.g. the Sybil attacks in cyberspace [37, 38], however, the connections amongst different malicious networks are actually very limited or none according to a latest observation [39]. A graph of connections among nodes can be established among the nodes in the mixed data set. Based on the graph we can obtain an adjacency matrix, which can be further transformed into the spectra space, where the nodes belong to the same botnet will establish a straight line in theory. As a result, we can accurately separate botnets in the spectra space.

We note that Big Data is an extremely hot topic at the moment. Obviously, the techniques from Big Data research are highly expected to address the problems in the problems that we mentioned in this subsection.

1.3.3 Topology Modelling of Malicious Networks

It is the toughest challenge to conduct topology modeling on the Internet and malicious networks. The topology of a network is a piece of critical information as physicists believe that structure determines functions. Therefore, it is especially important for us to understand the topology of botnets or other malicious networks. If we know the topology of a given botnet, then we can figure out the key nodes of the network. As a result, we can work with limited ISPs or organizations to fight against the botnet, e.g. terminate possible attacks or block communication path of bots.

However, so far our understanding in this aspect is extremely limited. The possible reason is that the data we have is usually "flat". For example, when we catched a malicious packet, we can only know its source IP address and destination address, however, the path from the source to the destination is usually hard to obtain.

Graph theory is a traditional and good tool for network topology modeling. Another popular method for network topology is network tomography [40, 41]. However, both of these methods study static graphs or networks. It is easy to notice that these tools are not sufficient to model the ever changing Internet or malicious networks. Moreover, we have to point out that majority of the current network models are loyal to their underneath physical network nodes and links. In our understanding, the following two directions are promising to explore on top of the traditional theories and tools.

- Logical topology. The current network topology models are loyalty to its physical networks, which may not reflect the truth of overlay networks, such as botnets. A logical model probably can represent a botnet more practically on top of the physical nodes and links.
- Dynamic graph. The traditional graph theory focuses on static graphs, however, the Internet or botnets are usually changing constantly. Therefore, it is necessary to inject dynamic elements into the classical graph theory to reflect the real situation of malicious networks or the Internet.

1.3.4 Dynamics of Malicious Networks

Botnet dynamics includes many aspects, the most important one is the number of bots of a given botnet against time, simply, the size of botnet. This information is valuable to defenders, as defenders can organize their defence and budget the cost better with this information in place.

There are some work on size of botnet. A direct method to count the number of bots is performance botnet infiltration to count bot IDs or IP addresses. Stone-Gross et al. [5] registered the URL of the Torpig botnet before the botmaster, therefore hijacked the *C&C* server for 10 days, and collected about 70 G data from the bots of Torpig botnet. They reported that the footprint of the Torpig botnet was 182,800, and the median and average size of the Torpig's live population was 49,272 and 48,532, respectively. They found 49,294 new infections during the 10 days takeover. Their research also indicated that the live population fluctuated periodically because of users switch between online and offline. Another method is DNS redirection. Dagon et al. [42] analyzed captured bots by honypot, identified the *C&C* server using the source code reverse engineering tools, manipulated the DNS entry, which was related to a botnet's IRC server, and redirected the DNS requests to a local sinkhole. They therefore were able to count the number of bots in a botnet. Their method counts the footprint of the botnet, and reported that the size of botnet (footprint) can reach 350,000. Rajab et al. [18] pointed out that it is inaccuracy of counting the unique IP addresses of bots, because of the DHCP and NAT techniques were employed extensively on the Internet ([5] confirms this by their observation that 78.9 % of the infected machines were behind a NAT, VPN, proxy, or firewall). They therefore proposed to examine the hits of DNS caches to find the lower bound of the size of a given botnet.

The main challenge of this field is: For a given botnet or malware and a given range of the network, what is the density of bot or malware in the network? There is plenty of research concerning the recruitment of malware networks based on epidemic theory [43, 44], however the research on malware or bot distribution is limited. To date, we only know that the distribution is non-uniform based on information theory [45], and the network topology has a big impact on the spread of malware [46].

The dominant tool for the size issue is the epidemic model, which is the major theory for biology virus propagation modeling, and is also used by computer scientists [43]. As the member recruitment of botnets is essentially the same as computer viruses, therefore, the usage of the epidemic theory looks effective to model the size of botnet. However, researchers have noticed that the current computer virus model lacks accuracy after the early stage of propagation [44].

As the botnet dynamics is mainly related with time, therefore, time series analysis methods are probably effective to address this problem. Many questions remain unanswered, e.g. periodicity, frequency of various bot recruitment and attacking activities; What is the distribution of a specific botnet or virus? How many of the Internet nodes have been compromised since the beginning of a botnet?

1.3.5 Concealed Malicious Activity Detection

There are many intrusion detection and virus detection algorithms in place [30, 31], but only limited detection algorithms on malicious activity throughout the current literature. We do not know how many illegal activities go undetected using current detection systems. The false negative rate is an essential challenge for us, since attackers are exhausting their efforts to disguise their malicious traces. In some cases, malicious bots demonstrate decent behaviour most of the time in order to fool our detection systems.

In order to address these issues, it is necessary to integrate understandings of human criminal behaviour with information techniques to reduce the false negative rate of detection as much as possible. For a long time, the network security community has focused on technology oriented methodologies, and ignored the human aspect of criminal behaviour, which greatly enhances our understanding of criminals. There are some work in this direction [33, 34]. The game theory [47] and social network technologies [37, 48] should be employed in the design of the detection algorithm of concealed malicious activities.

In particular, the following two aspects should be investigated.

1. Identifying the boundary of detection for a given level of security investment using game theory. It is obvious from the attackers' viewpoint that a high frequency of malicious activity results in a high probability of being detected. For example, frequent vulnerability scanning or sensitive data downloading will make the compromised computer stand out from its peers. There is a threshold at which malicious activity is far more prone to detection. Presently, the network security community has no conception of where this boundary lies. It is worthwhile to explore this bound between detectable and undetectable using game theory and identify the Nash Equilibrium (if it exists). With the bound information in hand, we can actually estimate the false negative probability in detection. With this information in place, researchers can develop a strict low false negative detection algorithm, which can push the threshold to a minimum, consequently suppressing the frequency of malicious activities.
2. Identifying malicious nodes using social network technologies. In general, we can divide all Internet based nodes into two groups, benign and malicious (e.g. members of one specific botnet). It has been proved that the communication among the nodes within each group is quite rich. However, there is much less communication among nodes from different groups. Therefore, for a given node, the probability that the node is malicious increases if the node has a certain amount of communication with the known malicious nodes.

1.3.6 Forensics of Malicious Networks

Cyber forensics is an attractive topic, and is extremely important as we have more and more killer applications in the cyberspace. However, the work on this field is not much. One solid topic is IP traceback, which refers to the capability of identifying the actual source of malicious packets sent across the Internet. Current methods of traceback rely on independent local networks with no global coordination. They are hence incapable of accurately tracing back cyber criminals at the Internet level. We can categorize the methods of IP traceback into three major groups: deterministic packet marking (DPM in short) [49–51], probabilistic packet marking (PPM in short) [52,53], and information theoretical based method [54]. The first strategy marks IP packets at the source local area network where the packets are generated, whereas the second strategy marks incoming packets at the edge routers of the local area network where the potential victim resides. Both of these strategies require routers to inject marks into individual packets. Moreover, the PPM strategy can only operate in a local range of the Internet (e.g. ISP networks), where the defender has the authority to manage. However, this kind of ISP networks is generally quite small, and we cannot traceback to the attack sources located out of the ISP network. The DPM strategy requires all the Internet routers to be updated for packet marking. However, with only 25 spare bits available in an IP version 4 packet, the scalability of DPM is a huge problem. Moreover, the DPM mechanism poses an extraordinary challenge on storage for packet logging for routers. Therefore, it is infeasible in practice at present. Further, both PPM and DPM are vulnerable to hacking, which is referred to as packet pollution. The third method measure the variation of flow entropy at routers to traceback to attack sources. It overcomes the disadvantages of the previous two, however it needs a global collaboration, which is hard to achieve.

Attack source inferring is an applicable method for today's cyber environment as direct traceback is almost impossible. In this case the Bayesian inference networks is probably a good choice. The research community desires to have effective and efficient tools to carry out cyber forensics tasks.

References

1. V. D. Gligor, "A note on denial-of-service in operating systems," *IEEE Transactions on Software Engineering*, vol. 10, no. 3, pp. 320–324, 1984.
2. T. Peng, C. Leckie, and K. Ramamohanarao, "Survey of network-based defense mechanisms countering the dos and ddos problems," *ACM Computing Survey*, vol. 39, no. 1, 2007.
3. V. L. L. Thing, M. Sloman, and N. Dulay, "A survey of bots used for distributed denial of service attacks," in *Proceedings of the SEC*, 2007, pp. 229–240.
4. K. Tsui, "Tutorial - virus (malicious agent)," University of Calgary, Tech. Rep. SENG 609.22, 2001.
5. B. Stone-Gross, M. Cova, L. Cavallaro, B. Gilbert, M. Szydlowski, R. Kemmerer, C. Kruegel, and G. Vigna, "Your botnet is my botnet: Analysis of a botnet takeover," in *Proceedings of the ACM conference on computer communication security*, 2009, pp. 635–647.
6. C. Y. Cho, J. Caballero, C. Grier, V. Paxson, and D. Song, "Insights from the inside: A view of botnet management from infiltration," in *Proceedings of USENIX LEET*, 2010.
7. M. H. Sqalli, F. Al-Haidari, and K. Salah, "Edos-shield - a two-steps mitigation technique against edos attacks in cloud computing," in *Proceedings of the UCC*, 2011, pp. 49–56.

8. J. Idziorek, M. Tannian, and D. Jacobson, "The insecurity of cloud utility models," *IT Professional*, vol. 15, no. 2, pp. 22–27, 2013.
9. R. Lua and K. C. Yow, "Mitigating ddos attacks with transparent and intelligent fast-flux swarm network," *IEEE Network*, no. July/August, pp. 28–33, 2011.
10. http://www.nap.edu/catalog/11516.html.
11. P. Erdos and A. Renyi, "On random graphs. i," *Publicationes Mathematicae*, vol. 6, pp. 290–297, 1959.
12. D. J. Watts and S. H. Strogatz, "Collective dynamics of 'small-world' networks," *Nature*, vol. 393, no. 6668, pp. 440–442, 1998.
13. A. L. Barabasi and R. Albert, "Emergence of scaling in random networks," *Science*, vol. 286, no. 5439, pp. 509–512, 1999.
14. R. Albert and A.-L. Barabasi, "Statistical mechanics of complex networks," *Reviews of Modern Physics*, vol. 74, pp. 47–97, 2002.
15. L. Breslau, P. Cao, L. Fan, G. Phillips, and S. Shenker, "Web caching and zipf-like distributions: Evidence and implications," in *Proceedings of the INFOCOM*, 1999, pp. 126–134.
16. M. E. Crovella and A. Bestavros, "Self-similarity in world wide web traffic: evidence and possible causes," *IEEE/ACM Transactions on Networking*, vol. 5, no. 6, pp. 835–846, 1997.
17. M. Bailey, E. Cooke, F. Jahanian, Y. Xu, and M. Karir, "A survey of botnet technology and defenses," in *Proceedings of the cybersecurity applications and technology conference for Homeland security*, 2009.
18. M. A. Rajab, J. Zarfoss, F. Monrose, and A. Terzis, "My botnet is bigger than yours (maybe, better than yours): why size estimates remain challenging," in *Proceedings of the first conference on First Workshop on Hot Topics in Understanding Botnets*. USENIX Association, 2007.
19. N. Ianelli and A. Hackworth, "Botnets as vehicle for online crime," in *Proceedings of the 18th Annual FIRST Conference*, 2006.
20. R. Perdisci, I. Corona, D. Dagon, and W. Lee, "Detecting malicious flux service networks through passive analysis of recursive dns traces," in *Proceedings of the Computer Security Applications Conference*, 2009, pp. 311–320.
21. N. Jiang, J. Cao, Y. Jin, L. Li, and Z.-L. Zhang, "Identifying suspicious activities through dns failure graph analysis," in *Proceedings of Network Protocols (ICNP)*, oct. 2010, pp. 144–153.
22. D. K. McGrath and M. Gupta, "Behind phishing: An examination of phisher modi operandi," in *Proceedings of the LEET*, 2008.
23. J. Ma, L. K. Saul, S. Savage, and G. M. Voelker, "Beyond blacklists: learning to detect malicious web sites from suspicious urls," in *Proceedings of the ACM SIGKDD*. ACM, 2009, pp. 1245–1254.
24. Y. Xie, F. Yu, K. Achan, R. Panigrahy, G. Hulten, and I. Osipkov, "Spamming botnets: signatures and characteristics," in *Proceedings of the SIGCOMM*, 2008, pp. 171–182.
25. G. Gu, P. Porras, V. Yegneswaran, M. Fong, and W. Lee, "BotHunter: Detecting malware infection through ids-driven dialog correlation," in *Proceedings of the 16th USENIX Security Symposium*, August 2007.
26. G. Gu, R. Perdisci, J. Zhang, and W. Lee, "BotMiner: Clustering analysis of network traffic for protocol- and structure-independent botnet detection," in *Proceedings of the 17th USENIX Security Symposium*, 2008.
27. D. Moore, C. Shannon, D. J. Brown, G. M. Voelker, and S. Savage, "Inferring internet denial-of-service activity," *ACM Transactions on Computer Systems*, vol. 24, no. 2, pp. 115–139, 2006.
28. http://www.wombat-project.org/.
29. http://www.planet-lab.org/.
30. W. Yu, X. Wang, X. Fu, D. Xuan, and W. Zhao, "An invisible localization attack to internet threat monitors," *IEEE Transactions on Parallel and Distributed Systems*, vol. 20, no. 11, pp. 1611–1625, 2009.

31. L. Huang, X. Nguyen, M. N. Garofalakis, J. M. Hellerstein, M. I. Jordan, A. D. Joseph, and N. Taft, "Communication-efficient online detection of network-wide anomalies," in *Proceedings of the INFOCOM*, 2007, pp. 134–142.

32. Y. Tsaig and D. L. Donoho, "Compressed sensing," *IEEE Transactions on Information Theory*, vol. 52, pp. 1289–1306, 2006.

33. S. Yu, W. Zhou, and R. Doss, "Information theory based detection against network behavior mimicking ddos attack," *IEEE Communications Letters*, vol. 12, no. 4, pp. 319–321, 2008.

34. S. Yu, W. Zhou, W. Jia, S. Guo, Y. Xiang, and F. Tang, "Discriminating ddos attacks from flash crowds using flow correlation coefficient," *IEEE Transactions on Parallel Distributed Systems*, vol. 23, no. 6, pp. 1073–1080, 2012.

35. R. Duda, P. Hart, and D. Stork, *Unsupervised learning and clustering*. Wiley, 2001.

36. P. Van Mieghem, *Graph Spectra for Complex Networks*. Cambridge press, 2011.

37. H. Yu, M. Kaminsky, P. B. Gibbons, and A. D. Flaxman, "Sybilguard: defending against sybil attacks via social networks," *IEEE/ACM Transactions on Networking*, vol. 16, no. 3, pp. 576–589, 2008.

38. H. Yu, C. Shi, M. Kaminsky, P. B. Gibbons, and F. Xiao, "Dsybil: Optimal sybil-resistance for recommendation systems," in *IEEE Symposium on Security and Privacy*, 2009, pp. 283–298.

39. Z. Yang, C. Wilson, X. Wang, B. Y. Zhao, and Y. Dai, "Uncovering social nework sybils in the wild," in *Internet Measurement Conference*, 2011.

40. K. Claffy, T. Monk, and D. McRobb, "Internet tomography," *Nature*, Jan 1999.

41. M. Coates, A. Hero, R. Nowak, and B. Yu, "Internet tomography," *IEEE Signal Processing Magazine*, vol. 19, pp. 47–65, 2002.

42. D. Dagon, C. Zou, and W. Lee, "Modeling botnet propagation using time zones," in *Proceedings of the 13th Network and Distributed System Security Symposium NDSS*, 2006.

43. P. De, Y. Liu, and S. K. Das, "An epidemic theoretic framework for vulnerability analysis of broadcast protocols in wireless sensor networks," *IEEE Transactions on Mobile Computing*, vol. 8, no. 3, pp. 413–425, 2009.

44. C. C. Zou, W. Gong, D. F. Towsley, and L. Gao, "The monitoring and early detection of internet worms," *IEEE/ACM Transactions on Networking*, vol. 13, no. 5, pp. 961–974, 2005.

45. Z. Chen and C. Ji, "An information-theoretic view of network-aware malware attacks," *IEEE Transactions on Information Forensics and Security*, vol. 4, no. 3, pp. 530–541, 2009.

46. P. V. Mieghem, J. Omic, and R. E. Kooij, "Virus spread in networks," *IEEE/ACM Transactions on Networking*, vol. 17, no. 1, pp. 1–14, 2009.

47. W. Yu and K. J. R. Liu, "Secure cooperation in autonomous mobile ad-hoc networks under noise and imperfect monitoring: A game-theoretic approach," *IEEE Transactions on Information Forensics and Security*, vol. 3, no. 2, pp. 317–330, 2008.

48. C. C. Yang, "Information sharing and privacy protection of terrorist or criminal social networks," *IEEE International Conference on Intelligence and Security Informatics*, pp. 40–45, 2008.

49. A. Belenky and N. Ansari, "Ip traceback with deterministic packet marking," *IEEE Communications Letters*, vol. 7, pp. 162–164, 2003.

50. D. Dean, M. Franklin, and A. Stubblefield, "An algebraic approach to ip traceback," in *ACM Transactions on Information and System Security*, 2001, pp. 3–12.

51. Y. Xiang, W. Zhou, and M. Guo, "Flexible deterministic packet marking: An ip traceback system to find the real source of attacks," *IEEE Transactions on Parallel and Distributed Systems*, vol. 20, no. 4, pp. 567–580, 2009.

52. B. Al-Duwairi and G. Manimaran, "Novel hybrid schemes employing packet marking and logging for ip traceback," *IEEE Transactions on Parallel and Distributed Systems*, vol. 17, no. 5, pp. 403–418, 2006.

53. M. T. Goodrich, "Probabilistic packet marking for large-scale ip traceback," *IEEE/ACM Transactions on Networking*, vol. 16, no. 1, pp. 15–24, 2008.

54. S. Yu, W. Zhou, R. Doss, and W. Jia, "Traceback of ddos attacks using entropy variations," *IEEE Transactions on Parallel and Distributed Systems*, vol. 22, no. 3, pp. 412–425, 2011.

Chapter 2
Malicious Networks for DDoS Attacks

Abstract In this chapter, we explore botnet, the engine of DDoS attacks, in cyberspace. We focus on two recent techniques that hackers are using to sustain their malicious networks, fast fluxing and domain fluxing. We present the mechanisms of these two techniques and also survey the detection and anti-attack methods that have been proposed against them in literature.

2.1 Introduction

Nowadays, there are numerous malicious attacks in the cyberspace. These attacks are pervasive in the Internet, and often cause great financial loss [1, 2]. Botnets are the engines behind majority of the attacks. A botnet is usually established by a botnet writer developing a program, called a bot or agent, and installing the program on compromised computers on the Internet using various techniques. All the bots from a botnet are controlled by a botmaster. The hosts running these programs are known as zombies [1, 3, 4]. For a botnet, there is one or a number of command and control (*C&C*) servers to communicate with bots and collect data from them. In order to disguise himself from legal forces, botmaster changes the URL of his *C&C* frequently, such as weekly. An excellent explanation about this could be found in [3].

Motivated by huge financial or political reward, attackers find it worthwhile to organize sophisticated botnets for use as attack tools. There are numerous types of botnets in cyberspace, such as DSNXbot, evilbot, G-Sysbot, sdbot, and Spybot [3]. On one hand, researchers have studied botnets from various perspectives, including botnet probing events [5], Internet connectivity [6], size [7], and domain fluxing [8, 9]. On the other hand, botnet owners have at their disposal state-of-the-art techniques, such as stepping stones, reflector, IP spoofing [1, 10], code obfuscation, memory encryption [11], and peer-to-peer implementation technology [10, 12, 13] to sustain their botnets and disguise their malicious activities and traces.

S. Yu, *Distributed Denial of Service Attack and Defense*, SpringerBriefs in Computer Science, DOI 10.1007/978-1-4614-9491-1_2, © The Author(s) 2014

A report from Symantec's MessageLabs shows 90.4 % of total emails were spam in June 2009. Among all spam, 83.2 % was sent through botnets. In addition, many spam emails included viruses, phishing attacks, and web-based malware. Therefore, sending spam through botnets can help to conduct further network attacks [14].

Researchers have applied signature-based methods to detect botnets for a long time. These signature-based techniques have been widely employed by some Honeynet projects, which has been discussed in [15, 16]. However, these methods cannot detect newly developed botnets as the signatures of new botnets are unknown or some botnets are polymorphic [17]. Some IRC-based approaches were developed to overcome this problem. For example, Binkley et al. [18] developed an anomaly based system combining IRC statistics and TCP work load, and Karasaridis et al. [19] applied a passive anomaly-based characterization methodology based on botnets behavior characteristics. However, these methods have high false positive rates [17].

Many researches focused on how to detect botnets or trace the botnet master. Meanwhile, many surveys reflected what had been done and summarized what future work should be. Feily et al. [20] surveyed botnet mechanisms and botnet detection techniques based on different classes they identified: signature-based, anomaly-based, DNS-based, and mining-based. They also compared and evaluated the advantages and disadvantages of some typical researches from each category.

However, in order to disguise their traces and malicious activities, botnet writers are exhausting their energy to design new strategies and mechanisms to fly under the radar. In this chapter, we discuss two recent advanced botnet mechanisms:

1. Fast Flux (FF in short): A mechanism that a set of IP addresses change frequently corresponding to a unique domain name.
2. Domain Flux (DF in short): A mechanism that a set of domain names are generated automatically and periodically corresponding to an URL of a *C&C* server.

2.2 The Fast Flux Mechanism and Detection

2.2.1 The Fast Flux Mechanism

Fast Flux (FF) is an earlier strategy employed by hackers to evade botnet detection. By IP fast flux, the mapping between multiple IP addresses and one single domain name is rapidly changing [21]. This technique makes it sophisticated to block or take down the C&C Server.

Networks that apply fast flux techniques are called fast fluxing network (FFN). Both legitimate or suspicious FFNs show almost the same characteristics, such as short TTLs and large IP pools [22]. Furthermore, fast flux can be classified into two categories: single flux and double flux.

In terms of single flux, a domain name may be resolved to different IPs in different time ranges. For example, a user accesses the same domain name twice in a short time period. For the first time, a bot sends a DNS query to the DNS server, which resolves that the corresponding IP address as IP_1. With IP_1 in place, the bot accesses a flux agent FA_1, which redirects the request to the real server "mothership". This "mothership" then processes the request and responds to FA_1. Finally, FA_1 relays the response back to the bot. After a short while, the same bot or other bots may access the same domain name again. However, the mapping between the domain name and IP_1 has been changed by hackers. As a result, a DNS server responses a different IP address, IP_2, to the name service request, and the bot uses this new address IP_2 to connect to another flux agent FA_2, which redirects the bot to the "mothership" [22].

The double flux is a more sophisticated method of counter detection compared with the single flux. It frequently changes both the flux agents and the registration in DNS servers. That is to say, in addition to fluxing their own agents, the authoritative domain name server is also a part of fluxing. This provides an additional layer of redundancy within malware networks. The fluxing nodes repeatedly register and de-register from the domain name system [21].

The fast fluxing network techniques have been abused by attackers to maintain their botnets. This is known as fast fluxing network attack (FFNA). In this case, almost all compromised computers become fluxing agents. Agents can be added or removed from the agent pool dynamically; thus, any mechanism that tends to block agents cannot take down the whole botnet [23].

2.2.2 Fast Flux Detection

Holz et al. [24] claimed that they were the first to develop a metric to detect fast flux service network (FFSN) empirically. They identified three possible parameters that could be used to distinguish normal network behaviors from that of FFSNs: the number of IP-domain mappings in all DNS lookups, the number of nameserver records in one single domain lookup, and the number of autonomous system in all IP-domain pairs. Based on these three parameters, they defined a metric, flux-score, which was a result of a linear decision function to detect FFSNs. A higher score indicated a higher fluxing degree, and vice versa. They evaluated their metric by a tenfold validation using a 2-month observation data set. Results showed that their method was able to distinguish normal network behavior from FFSN with a very low false positive probability.

There exist some limitations of these detection methods that focus on detecting domains that are related to IP addresses with short TTL in DNS query results [24,25]. In 2009, Zhou et al. [23] overcame these limitations by applying a behavior analysis model. To achieve this, they began with characterizing the behaviors of FF domains at some locations around these FF domains. Based on the analysis of those behaviors, they presented an analytical model, which showed the number of DNS

queries required to confirm an FF domain. In addition, they speeded up the detection
by two schemes. The first scheme was to associate IP addresses with the queries'
results from multiple DNS servers; the second scheme was to correlate queries'
results with multiple possible FF domains. They also proved that the detection
speed had been speeded up because of those correlation schemes. To avoid single
point of failure and improve the scalability, they developed a collaborative intrusion
detection architecture, LarSID, to support the distributed correlation using a peer-
to-peer publish-subscribe mechanism for evidence sharing. Their results showed
that their decentralized model was 16–10,000 times faster than previous centralized
model [25] with the same correlation schemes [23].

Caglayan et al. [26] developed a real-time detection model for fast flux service
networks (FFSN). They proposed to monitor the DNS activity of a web site at the
minute level using both active and passive methods in a distributed fashion. The
model included three key components: sensors, FF monitor database, and fast flux
monitor (FFM). For the first key component, there were three kinds of sensors:
active sensors, passive sensors, and analytic sensors. Active sensors were designed
to monitor several indicating parameters including TTL, FF activity index, and
footprint index. Passive sensors, however, were just functional replication of active
FFM sensors by leveraging DNS replication services. Analytic sensors were mainly
responsible for checking whether the IP addresses used by a certain web site existing
in a blacklist.

The FF monitor database was designed to record information, such as known
FFSNs, zombie IPs, collected from the sensors. By analyzing the data in the
FFM database, some analytical knowledge was able to be harvested. For example,
the size of FFSNs, growth rate estimation, social network of a FFSN where IP
addresses were shared by diverse FFSNs, footprints of a FFSN for a given ISP in
a given country, and so on. Finally, they developed a FFM classifier, which applied
a Bayesian belief network to integrate multiple active and passive sensors. This
classifier was then trained to calculate a prediction confidence. They demonstrated
empirically how their model can generate report to assist security analysts to
evaluate the security of a web site with acceptable accuracies. To improve the
detection accuracy, the model calculated decisions every 10 min. The more sampling
performed, the higher accuracy it obtains [26].

Perdisci et al. [27] developed a recursive DNS (RDNS) tracing methodology to
detect malicious flux service networks in the wild. In their model, a sensor was
deployed in front of the RDNS server, and passively monitored DNS traffic and
stored information from a FF domains into a centralized data collector. Furthermore,
to aim on botnets, they developed pre-filtering rules that were used to identify
malicious FF networks. They considered a network as malicious FF network by
four characteristics (short TTL, the change rate of the set of resolved IPs returned
from each query, a large number of resolved IPs, and resolved IPs scattered across
different networks). Based on these rules, they developed filters to gather the traffic
they required. Besides, the filters in the sensors stored historic information. Different
from most previous works, they conducted a fine-grained analysis on collected data.
Firstly, they clustered domains with high relations based on their common features.

Secondly, the clusters of the domains were then classified according to the resolved IP addresses. Finally, they applied a statistical supervised learning method to build a network classifier to distinguish malicious flux services from legitimate ones. Results indicated that their model was able to distinguish and classify malicious and benign FF networks clearly.

Yu et al. [22] pointed out that one critical step of detecting botnet fast flux was to distinguish the fast fluxing attack network (FFAN) from benign fast fluxing service network (FFSN). Their idea was an improvement of the method discussed in [24], which was not able to distinguish benign ones from malicious ones. They identified FFAN by observing the agent lifespan. They showed that all agents in FFSN should keep alive almost 24/7. However, the alive time of FFAN bots is unpredictable to some extent, because the compromised computers cannot be controlled by FFAN master physically. Based on this lifespan difference between FFSN and FFAN, the authors proposed two metrics and developed a monitoring system. The first metric they defined was the average online rate (AOR), which was measured once per hour within a 24 h time interval. The AOR of FFSN should be close to 100 %. However, FFAN fluxing agents (bots) were out of attackers' control, thus the AOR was usually far bellow the AOR of FFSN. The second metric was the minimum available rate (MAR), which was the result of the number of times available out of the total measured times. For the same reason, the MAR of FFAN was far lower than that of FFSN. Based on the two metrics, they developed a flux agent monitoring system consisting mainly of four components. A digging tool was developed to gather information and add new IPs into IP record database. The second part was the agent monitor that sent HTTP request to the IPs in the IP record database and stored the responses. The third one was the IP lifespan record database storing the service status: 1 for available service, and 0 for unavailable service. The last key component was a detector differentiating FFAN from FFSN by IP lifepan records and the two metrics. Experimental results demonstrated that their system was able to distinguish FFAN from FFSN clearly because all benign FFSN had high and stable AOR and MAR, but that of the FFAN were much lower and less stable.

2.3 The Domain Flux Mechanism and Detection

Due to a single domain name, fast flux has a disadvantage of single point failure once fluxing is identified. Therefore, hackers developed a more survivable mechanism: domain flux.

2.3.1 The Domain Flux Mechanism

Stone-Gross et al. [3] pointed out that some recent botnet programs, such as Torpig, were using domain flux to sustain their botnets. Inspired by [28–30], they discussed domain-generation techniques and provided a research report on how they cooperated with FBI to take over an advanced domain flux based botnet [3].

Domain flux is based on the idea of generating domain names through a domain generation algorithm (DGA). Both *C&C* server and its bots follow the same algorithm seeded by the same value to obtain consistent dynamic domain names. Bots try to contact the *C&C* server and other servers controlled by the botnet master according to a domain list until one DNS query succeeds. If the current domain has been blocked or suspended by authorities, bots will try to calculate other domain names using the DGA. The key idea is that the algorithm must make sure that all bots can generate domains by the same seed. Stone-gross and the co-authors revealed that Torpig calculated sub-domains using the current week and year first but independent of the current day, and then appended the top level domain (TLD). The domains generated might be "weekyear.com" or "weekyear.biz", and so on. At the same time, the bots will use these auto-generated domain names to contact the *C&C* server. If failed, bots will use the day information to calculate the "daily domain", such as "day.com" or "day.net", etc. If all these domains cannot be resolved, bots will try to use the hard-coded domain names in a configuration file as the last option [3].

2.3.2 Domain Flux Detection

It is critical for bots to phone "home" using the domain flux technique for botnet writers; it is also important for defenders to use this key component to defeat botnets. There have been sufficient work in domain flux detection and botnet takeover.

In 2009, Stone-Gross et al. conducted an in-depth research on taking over the real world Torpig botnet [3]. Taking advantage of reverse engineering on domain generation algorithm (DGA) of Torpig, they revealed that Torpig owners will not pre-register all possible domains in advance. Therefore, they registered the related domain name of *C & C* server of Torpig before the botnet owners. As a result, they took over the botnet for about 10 days. The bots of Torpig treated their server as the *C & C* server. The authors recorded many information about the botnet. They estimated the size of the Torpig by counting node identifiers (N_{id}) that were unique in Torpig. They also analyzed the advantages of the method by comparing to IP count that could be misled by DHCP. Their method was quite different from previous works in [7] and [31]. Rajab et al. [7] focused on detecting the size of IRC-based botnets by querying DNS server caches to estimate the number of bots who had connected the C&C server. Kanich et al. [31] worked on detecting the size of P2P storm networks using active probing and crawling the over-net distributed hash table (DHT).

Ma et al. [32] applied a supervised machine learning method to detect and prevent users from visiting malicious web sites based on automated URL classification. It was a lightweight model that investigated the lexical features and host-based properties of malicious URLs. The lexical features that they selected were the length of entire URL, and the number of dots in the URL with of a bag-of-words representation. For host-based features, they extracted IP address properties, WHOIS (registrars) properties, domain name properties (e.g., TTL), and geographic properties (physical location, link speed, and so on). To train and evaluate the features, they applied three classification models – Naive Bayes, Support Vector Machine (SVM), and Logistic Regression on data sets from four different sources (two malicious and two legitimate). They found that WHOIS and lexical features were able to provide rich information. Moreover, the combination of all features to form a full feature set could reach the highest detection accuracy. To compare full feature performance with traditional blacklist method, they used a ROC graph to explain how full feature made the difference. At last, they showed how their classifiers selected automatically from large amount of features and determined the most predictive ones and achieved a modest false positive rate.

Later in 2009, Ma et al. [33] developed an online learning approach based on the same two groups of features from their previous work [32]. Compared with the previous study, the new model could identify suspicious URLs over time by a live feed of labeled URLs from a large web mail provider. Live feed made this model more appropriate for online learning and processing on large number of URLs. They also pointed out and demonstrated that continuous feed of new features was the key to detect new malicious URLs. For their feature selection, lexical and host-based types accounted for 62 and 38 %, respectively. They progressed the online learning with two steps. Firstly, they designed a sequence of feature-vector label pairs. The algorithm made a label prediction by a linear classifier. After obtaining actual labels from prediction, the algorithm checked it with the labels in the feature-vector label pairs. If they did not match, the algorithm would record it as an error.

Ma et al.'s online method was a combination of classical and recent algorithms including four sub-algorithms. The first sub-algorithm was perception by which linear classifier made update to a weighted vector when there were any mistakes. The second one is a method of applying stochastic gradient descent to logistic regression. This method provided an online means to optimize an objective function and approximated the gradient of the original objective. The objective function was defined as a sum of the samples' individual objective functions, and the model parameters were updated incrementally by the gradients of individual objectives. The third sub-algorithm was the passive-aggressive algorithm, which was used to make a minimum change to correct any mistakes and low-confidence predictions. The last sub-algorithm was confidence-weighted (CW) algorithm by which less confident weights are updated more aggressively than high confident ones. It also modeled uncertainties in weights using a Gaussian distribution to describe the per-feature confidence. CW could perform a fine-grained distinction among all features' weight confidence. Therefore it was appropriate for detecting malicious URLs as long as dynamic features can be constantly introduced. Finally, they obtained a high detection accuracy up to 99 % over a balanced data set [33].

In 2010, Jiang et al. [34] proposed a light-weight anomaly detection approach using DNS failure graphs based on failed DNS queries. They captured all interactions between hosts and unresolvable domain names, which could be considered as auto-generated domains used by botnets. Edges are represented as associations between hosts and domains. They learnt from previous studies that failed DNS queries come from a small portion of human errors and mis-configurations [35], and a large part of it were generated from malicious activities [36, 37]. In a botnet, as all bots use the same algorithm to generate sub-domains, the queries for these domains will attribute to correlated failures, which construct density subgraphs in a DNS failure graph. They believed that such subgraphs would show some interaction patterns. To confirm their assumption, they gathered DNS query data from several major DNS servers in a large campus network for 3 months. After that, they recursively decomposed the DNS failure graph, and extracted dense subgraphs by applying a statistical graph decomposition technique, which is an extension of the tri-nonnegative matrix factorization (TNMF) algorithm [38]. By analyzing the structure properties, they classified the subgraphs into three categories: host-star, DNS-star, and bi-mesh. By referring to some external data sources, such as domain name blacklists, they found that bi-mesh structures, where a group of hosts are strongly associated with a group of domains, reflect botnet activities [34].

Later, Prakash et al. [39] developed a Phishnet to protect system from phishing attacks. As shown in the Symantec's MessageLabs report [14], 83.2 % spam was sent through botnets in June 2009. Thus, Phishnet should be able to detect auto-generated domain names of those spam sent through botnets. This is a blacklisting-based method, which was improved to overcome the limitations of traditional blacklisting methods. They pointed out that it was easy to evade URL blacklisting because blacklisting methods perform exact matching between target URLs and entries in the list. Two key components in their model can help to overcome this limitation. In the first component, there are five heuristics to enumerate simple combinations of known phishing URLs to discover new phishing sites. It works in an offline fashion, examines current blacklists, and generates new URLs based on these heuristics systematically. It was also responsible for confirming whether the new generated URLs are indeed malicious through DNS queries and content matching in an automatic fashion. The five heuristics came from URL lexical similarities and their own observations in the PhishTank database. They studied these five heuristics to generate new URLs from existing Phishing URLs in a blacklist. The first heuristic was to replace the top-level domains (TLD). The second one was the IP address equivalence, which meant that they clustered phishing URLs by close IP addresses. Then, they created new URLs by combining different host names and pathnames in the same clusters. The third heuristic was the directory structure similarity. They believed that similar pathes might attribute to similar sets of file names. Therefore, they grouped directories with similar structures, and then exchanged the filenames among URLs within the same group. The fourth one was query string substitution. For similar URLs, they exchanged the queried content string which was after the question mark in an URL. The last heuristic was the brand name equivalence. Some URLs use the same URL structure but different brand names. To confirm their heuristics, the existence of those generated child URLs were tested by a verification process. By DNS lookups, the URLs that were not able to be resolved would be filtered out. For resolved URLs, the model would establish connections to the corresponding servers first and then took advantage of HTTP GET method to retrieve content from it. If the status code was 200/202 (successful), a content similarity would be computed between the parent and child URLs. The second component was an approximate matching algorithm, which performed an approximate match of a new URL against an existing blacklist. The algorithm performed the match by measuring the syntactic and semantic variations. To achieve this, the algorithm broke the input URLs into four different entities – IP address, host name, directory structure and brand name. Each individual entity would be scored and then a final score would be computed by combining all individual scores. If the final score exceeded a certain threshold, the URL would be marked as suspicious. They showed that the system could keep the false negative rate under 3 %, and false positive rate under 5 %.

Yadav et al. [40] researched how to investigate alphanumeric unigrams and bigrams (two consecutive characters) to identify domains generated algorithmically. They were motivated by the observation that auto-generated domains are quite different from legitimate ones in terms of spelling or pronounceable features. They developed a few detection metrics based on signal detection theory and statistical learning technique. Their method focused on detecting domains generated from pseudo-random string generation algorithms and dictionary base generators, which produced pronounceable words that were not in English dictionaries. Following that, they implemented their model in two parts. Firstly, they grouped DNS queries by Top Level Domain (TLD), IP-addresses they were mapped to, or the connected component they belonged to. Secondly, they used the metrics to characterize the distribution of the alphanumeric characters or bigrams. They employed three metrics (the KL-distance, the Jaccard index, and the edit distance) to distinguish a set of legitimate domain names from malicious ones. They also performed in-depth per-domain analysis, per-IP analysis, and component analysis to evaluate the performance. Through the experiments, they found that Jaccard index metric performed the best, followed by the edit distance measurement and the KL divergence. They highlighted that their methodology was able to be used to detect unknown and unclassified botnets.

2.4 Modelling Malicious Networks

The model for network virus infection and curing has been explored extensively. Based on epidemiology research, Zou et al. [41] proposed a number of models for monitoring and *early* detection of Internet worms. As they pointed that this kind of models are appropriate for a system that consists of a large number of vulnerable hosts; in other words, the model is effective at the *early* stage of the outbreaks of virus, and the accuracy of the model drops otherwise. There are a few assumptions in this model as follows.

1. There are only two possible states for a given node in the network, healthy or infected.
2. The nodes stay in the system forever, and there is no curing process.

As a variant of the epidemic category, Sellke et al. [42] proposed a stochastic branching process model for characterizing the propagation of Internet worms, the model especially focuses on the number of compromised computers against the number of worm scans, and presented a close form expression for this relationship.

Dagon et al. [43] extended the model of [41] by introducing with time zone information $\alpha(t)$, and built a model describe the impact on number of live members of botnets with diurnal effect. The impact of side information on the spreading behavior of network virus is also explored, such as the topology network information [44–46], distribution of vulnerable hosts [47], and they are more focus on the life circle of infections in theory.

The features of peer-to-peer networks have been explored extensively [48–50]. Stutzbach and Rajaie studied the three different p2p systems that are widely deployed, unstructured file-sharing system(Gnutella), content-distribution system (BitTorrent) and distributed hash table (Kad), and they found that the group-level properties of the dynamics exhibit similar behavior across all three applications, although there are difference in terms of per-peer properties. The long term observation on the KAD peer-to-peer network from Steiner et al. also confirms the findings in [49].

As we have seen, the epidemic models are current the mainstream methods for virus or malicious network in cyberspace. We therefore present the basic concepts of epidemic modelling in this subsection. We refer interested readers to [51] and [52], and recent development could be find in some dedicated journals, such as, Elsevier's Mathematical Biocience.

Epidemic theory has a long history in study of biological infectious diseases. In the 1930s, Kermack and McKendrick published a series of papers titled "Contributions to the mathematical theory of epidemics". These papers are often seen as the basis of further research in mathematical modeling of the spread of infectious diseases. Depending on different assumptions and scenarios, we usually have different epidemic models, such as the naive model, the susceptible-infectious model (SI in short), the susceptible-infectious-susceptible model (SIS in short), and the susceptible-infectious-recovery model (SIR in short).

In general, there are three different states for each individual in epidemic modeling: susceptible (S state), infectious (I state), or recovered (R state). Any individual of a studied population stays in one of the states. The susceptible individuals are those who have not been infected, but could be infected; the infected individuals are those who have the capability of spreading a disease; and the recovered individuals are those who used to be infected by a disease, but they have been cured.

2.4.1 The SI Model

In this model, we suppose that the total population is finite, and denoted as N; There is no curing process for the disease. The dynamics is described as follows.

$$\frac{dI_t}{dt} = \beta I_t(N - I_t), \tag{2.1}$$

where I_t is the infected hosts at time t, and β is the *pairwise rate of infection* in epidemic theories. The solution of Eq. (2.1) is

$$I_t = I_0 \cdot e^{\beta N t}, \tag{2.2}$$

where I_0 is the initial infected hosts.

The discrete form of this model is as follows.

$$I_t = (1 + \alpha \Delta)I_{t-1} - \beta \Delta I_{t-1}^2, \tag{2.3}$$

where Δ is the unit of time, and $\alpha(\alpha = \beta N)$ is the *infection rate*, which presents the average number of vulnerable hosts that can be infected by one infected host per time unit.

2.4.2 The SIS Model

In SIS epidemic model, there is a curing process. An infected individual can be cured, but it does not develop immunity to the disease. As a result, it could be infected again. In terms of states, a cured individual stays in the susceptible state. It is also assumed that there is no vertical transmission of the disease (all individuals are born susceptible) and there are no disease-related deaths. We assume that the birth rate equals the death rate, so that the total population size is constant. Let β be the infection rate, and α be the recovery rate. Therefore, the differential equations describing the dynamics of an SIS epidemic model are

$$\begin{cases} \frac{dS}{dt} = -\beta SI + \alpha I \\ \\ \frac{dI}{dt} = \beta SI - \alpha I \end{cases} \tag{2.4}$$

If we assume that the birth rate does not equal the death rate, then the size of the total population is variable. Let λ be the birth rate, then we have the dynamics as follows.

$$\begin{cases} \frac{dS}{dt} = -\frac{\beta SI}{N} + (\alpha + \lambda)I \\[2mm] \frac{dI}{dt} = \frac{\beta SI}{N} - (\alpha + \lambda)I \\[2mm] N = S + I \end{cases} \tag{2.5}$$

2.4.3 The SIR Model

In the SIR epidemic model, when individuals become infected, they develop immunity, and will not be infected in the future, and enter the immune state R. The SIR epidemic model has been applied to childhood diseases, such as chickenpox, measles, and mumps. The differential equations describing the dynamics of a SIR epidemic model are

$$\begin{cases} \frac{dS}{dt} = -\beta SI \\[2mm] \frac{dI}{dt} = \beta SI - \alpha I \\[2mm] \frac{dR}{dt} = \alpha I \end{cases} \tag{2.6}$$

If we assume that the birth rate does not equal the death rate, then the size of the total population is variable. Similarly, let λ be the birth rate, the previous model becomes

$$\begin{cases} \frac{dS}{dt} = -\frac{\beta SI}{N} + \lambda(I + R) \\[2mm] \frac{dI}{dt} = \frac{\beta SI}{N} - (\alpha + \lambda)I \\[2mm] \frac{dR}{dt} = \alpha I - \lambda R \\[2mm] N = S + I + R \end{cases} \tag{2.7}$$

Deterministic models are the first and popular tools, which are represented by differential equations of various forms. It is assumed that the size of susceptible and infectious population is a definite function of time in these models. These models can describe the dynamical inter-relations among the rates of change and population sizes. The mathematical theories for this type of models are well developed, and they are suitable for making predictions.

Of course, these three models are only a small part of epidemic modelling. There are plenty of modelling methodologies, such as stochastic based modelling, random graph based modelling. Interested readers can search for related references.

References

1. T. Peng, C. Leckie, and K. Ramamohanarao, "Survey of network-based defense mechanisms countering the dos and ddos problems," *ACM Computing Survey*, vol. 39, no. 1, 2007.
2. M. Edman and B. Yener, "On anonymity in an electronic society: A survey of anonymous communication systems," *ACM Computing Survey*, vol. 42, no. 1, 2009.
3. B. Stone-Gross, M. Cova, L. Cavallaro, B. Gilbert, M. Szydlowski, R. Kemmerer, C. Kruegel, and G. Vigna, "Your botnet is my botnet: Analysis of a botnet takeover," in *Proceedings of the ACM conference on computer communication security*, 2009, pp. 635–647.
4. C. Y. Cho, J. Caballero, C. Grier, V. Paxson, and D. Song, "Insights from the inside: A view of botnet management from infiltration," in *Proceedings of USENIX LEET*, 2010.
5. Z. Li, A. Goyal, Y. Chen, and V. Paxson, "Towards situational awareness of large-scale botnet probing events," *IEEE Transactions on Information Forensics and Security*, vol. 6, no. 1, pp. 175–188, 2011.
6. C. A. Shue, A. J. Kalafut, and M. Gupta, "Abnormally malicious autonomous systems and their internet connectivity," *IEEE/ACM Transactions on Networking*, vol. 20, no. 1, pp. 220–230, 2012.
7. M. A. Rajab, J. Zarfoss, F. Monrose, and A. Terzis, "My botnet is bigger than yours (maybe, better than yours): why size estimates remain challenging," in *Proceedings of the first conference on Hot Topics in Understanding Botnets*, 2007.
8. N. Jiang, J. Cao, Y. Jin, L. E. Li, and Z.-L. Zhang, "Identifying suspicious activities through dns failure graph analysis," in *Proceedings of the IEEE International Conference on Network Protocols*, 2010, pp. 144–153.
9. S. Yadav, A. K. K. Reddy, A. L. N. Reddy, and S. Ranjan, "Detecting algorithmically generated malicious domain names," in *Proceedings of the Internet Measurement Conference*, 2010, pp. 48–61.
10. V. L. L. Thing, M. Sloman, and N. Dulay, "A survey of bots used for distributed denial of service attacks," in *Proceedings of the SEC*, 2007, pp. 229–240.
11. N. Ianelli and A. Hackworth, "Botnets as vehicle for online crime," in *Proceedings of the 18th Annual FIRST Conference*, 2006.
12. P. Wang, S. Sparks, and C. C. Zou, "An advanced hybrid peer-to-peer botnet," *IEEE Transactions on Dependable and Secure Computing*, vol. 7, no. 2, pp. 113–127, 2010.
13. M. Bailey, E. Cooke, F. Jahanian, Y. Xu, and M. Karir, "A survey of botnet technology and defenses," in *Proceedings of the cybersecurity applications and technology conference for Homeland security*, 2009.
14. Symantec, "Cutwails bounce-back; instant messages can lead to instant malware," http://www.messagelabs.com/mlireport, 2009.
15. P. Bacher, T. Holz, M. Kotter, and G. Wicherski, "Know your enemy: Tracking botnets," http://www.honeynet.org/papers/bots, 2008.
16. Y. Tang and S. Chen, "Defending against internet worms: a signature-based approach," in *Proceedings of the INFOCOM*, 2005, pp. 1384–1394.
17. C. Li, W. Jiang, and X. Zou, "Botnet: Survey and case study," in *Proceedings of the ICICIC*, 2009, pp. 1184–1187.
18. J. R. Binkley and S. Singh, "An algorithm for anomaly-based botnet detection," in *Proceedings of the 2nd conference on Steps to Reducing Unwanted Traffic on the Internet – Volume 2*. USENIX Association, 2006.
19. A. Karasaridis, B. Rexroad, and D. Hoeflin, "Wide-scale botnet detection and characterization," in *Proceedings of the first conference on First Workshop on Hot Topics in Understanding Botnets*. USENIX Association, 2007.
20. M. Feily, A. Shahrestani, and S. Ramadass, "A survey of botnet and botnet detection," in *Proceedings of the SECURWARE*, June 2009, pp. 268–273.
21. Honeynet, "How fast-flux service network work," http://www.honeynet.org/node/132, 2008.

22. S. Yu, S. Zhou, and S. Wang, "Fast-flux attack network identification based on agent lifespan," in *Proceedings of the WCNIS*, June 2010, pp. 658 –662.
23. C. V. Zhou, C. Leckie, and S. Karunasekera, "Collaborative detection of fast flux phishing domains," *Journal of Networks*, vol. 4, no. 1, pp. 75–84, 2009.
24. T. Holz, C. Gorecki, K. Rieck, and F. C. Freiling, "Measuring and detecting fast-flux service networks," in *Proceedings of the NDSS*, 2008.
25. C. V. Zhou, C. Leckie, S. Karunasekera, and T. Peng, "A Self-healing, Self-protecting, Collaborative Intrusion Detection Architecture to Trace-back Fast-flux Phishing Domains," in *Proceedings of the 2nd IEEE Workshop on Autonomic Communication and Network Management*, Apr. 2008.
26. A. Caglayan, M. Toothaker, D. Drapeau, D. Burke, and G. Eaton, "Real-time detection of fast flux service networks," in *Proceedings of Homeland Security*, 2009, pp. 285–292.
27. R. Perdisci, I. Corona, D. Dagon, and W. Lee, "Detecting malicious flux service networks through passive analysis of recursive dns traces," in *Proceedings of the Computer Security Applications Conference*, 2009, pp. 311–320.
28. P. Amini, "Kraken botnet infiltration," http://dvlabs.tippingpoint.com/blog/2008/04/28/kraken-botnet-infiltration, 2008.
29. P. Porras, H. Saidi, and V. Yegneswaran, "A foray into conficker's logic and rendezvous points," in *Proceedings of the LEET*, 2009.
30. J. Wolf, "Technical details of srizbi's domain generation algorithm," http://blog.fireeye.com/research/2008/11/technical-details-of-srizbis-domain-generation-algorithm.html, 2008.
31. C. Kanich, K. Levchenko, B. Enright, G. M. Voelker, and S. Savage, "The heisenbot uncertainty problem: Challenges in separating bots from chaff." in *Proceedings of the LEET*. USENIX Association, 2008.
32. J. Ma, L. K. Saul, S. Savage, and G. M. Voelker, "Beyond blacklists: learning to detect malicious web sites from suspicious urls," in *Proceedings of the ACM SIGKDD*. ACM, 2009, pp. 1245–1254.
33. S. S. Justin Ma, Lawrence Saul and G. Voelker, "Identifying suspicious urls: An application of large-scale online learning," in *In Proc. of the International Conference on Machine Learning (ICML)*, 2009.
34. N. Jiang, J. Cao, Y. Jin, L. Li, and Z.-L. Zhang, "Identifying suspicious activities through dns failure graph analysis," in *Proceedings of Network Protocols (ICNP)*, oct. 2010, pp. 144–153.
35. V. Pappas, D. Wessels, D. Massey, S. Lu, A. Terzis, and L. Zhang, "Impact of configuration errors on dns robustness," *Selected Areas in Communications, IEEE Journal*, vol. 27, pp. 275–290, 2009.
36. Z. Zhu, V. Yegneswaran, and Y. Chen, "Using failure information analysis to detect enterprise zombies." in *SecureComm*, vol. 19. Springer, 2009, pp. 185–206.
37. D. Plonka and P. Barford, "Context-aware clustering of dns query traffic," in *Proceedings of the 8th ACM SIGCOMM conference on Internet measurement*. ACM, 2008, pp. 217–230.
38. Y. Jin, E. Sharafuddin, and Z. L. Zhang, "Unveiling core network-wide communication patterns through application traffic activity graph decomposition," in *Proceedings of the 11th international joint conference on Measurement and modeling of computer systems*. ACM, 2009, pp. 49–60.
39. P. Prakash, M. Kumar, R. Kompella, and M. Gupta, "Phishnet: Predictive blacklisting to detect phishing attacks," in *Proceedings of the INFOCOM*, 2010, pp. 1–5.
40. S. Yadav, A. K. K. Reddy, A. N. Reddy, and S. Ranjan, "Detecting algorithmically generated malicious domain names," in *Proceedings of the 10th annual conference on Internet measurement*. ACM, 2010, pp. 48–61.
41. C. C. Zou, W. Gong, D. F. Towsley, and L. Gao, "The monitoring and early detection of internet worms," *IEEE/ACM Transactions on Networking*, vol. 13, no. 5, pp. 961–974, 2005.
42. S. H. Sellke, N. B. Shroff, and S. Bagchi, "Modeling and automated containment of worms," *IEEE Transactions on Dependable and Secure Computing*, vol. 5, no. 2, pp. 71–86, 2008.
43. D. Dagon, C. Zou, and W. Lee, "Modeling botnet propagation using time zones," in *Proceedings of the 13th Network and Distributed System Security Symposium NDSS*, 2006.

44. A. J. Ganesh, L. Massoulié, and D. F. Towsley, "The effect of network topology on the spread of epidemics," in *Proceedings of the INFOCOM*, 2005, pp. 1455–1466.

45. J. Omic, A. Orda, and P. V. Mieghem, "Protecting against network infections: A game theoretic perspective," in *Proceedings of the INFOCOM*, 2009.

46. P. V. Mieghem, J. Omic, and R. Kooij, "Virus spread in networks," *IEEE/ACM Transactions on Networking*, vol. 17, no. 1, pp. 1–14, 2009.

47. Z. Chen and C. Ji, "An information-theoretic view of network-aware malware attacks," *IEEE Transactions on Information Forensics and Security*, vol. 4, no. 3, pp. 530–541, 2009.

48. M. Steiner, T. En-Najjary, and E. W. Biersack, "Long term study of peer behavior in the kad dht," *IEEE Transactions on Networking*, vol. 17, no. 5, pp. 1371–1384, 2009.

49. D. Stutzbach and R. Rejaie, "Understanding churn in peer-to-peer networks," in *Proceedings of the Internet Measurement Conference*, 2006, pp. 189–202.

50. S. Sen and J. Wang, "Analyzing peer-to-peer traffic across large networks," *IEEE/ACM Transactions on Networking*, vol. 12, no. 2, pp. 219–232, 2004.

51. D. J. Daley and J. Gani, *Epidemic Modelling: An Introduction*. Cambridge University Press, 1999.

52. N. Bailey, *The Mathematical Theory of Epidemics*. John Wiley & Sons, 1957.

Chapter 3
DDoS Attack Detection

Abstract In this chapter, we study on detection methods on DDoS attacks, which covers feature based detection methods, network traffic based detection methods, and detections against legitimate network event mimicking attacks. Each detection method is mathematically modelled for readers for possible further work in the fields.

3.1 Introduction

To defend against DDoS attacks, researchers have designed and implemented various countermeasures. In general, these countermeasures consist of three components: detection [1–6], defense (or mitigation) [3, 7–10], and IP trace back [11–13]. Among all the three categories, detection of DDoS attacks is obviously the first and the most important step in fighting against DDoS attacks.

In general, DDoS detection methods include activity profiling [14, 15], packet filtering [16, 17], sequential change-point detection [1, 2], wavelet analysis [18, 19], and so forth. All these methods are based on specific features or fingerprints of DDoS attacks. Unfortunately, it is very easy for hackers to simulate the features of legitimate network traffic to fool detection algorithms. For example, due to the open architecture of the Internet, hackers can spoof the source IP addresses of attack packets according to the real Internet IP address distribution to disable the source address distribution based detection algorithms [20, 21]. Attackers can also change the TTL value of attack packets according to the real hop distance between bots and the victim in order to fool the hop-count detection methods [2, 21]. In addition to these, attackers also mimic the behavior of flash crowds [1, 22], which are sudden increases of legitimate traffic, to disguise their attacks.

The majority of current DDoS detection methods are based on specific attack features [2, 4–6], and therefore, are passive and incapable of detecting new attacks. The entropy of attack flows is an independent method from specific attack features. The entropy detector mentioned in the survey [22] came from [14], which has

S. Yu, *Distributed Denial of Service Attack and Defense*, SpringerBriefs in Computer Science, DOI 10.1007/978-1-4614-9491-1_3, © The Author(s) 2014

the potential to raise the alarm for a crowd access, however, it is incapable of discriminating DDoS attacks from the surge of legitimate accesses (e.g., flash crowds). Lee and Xiang used relative entropy to measure the similarity of a known attack set and the suspected data set [23]. However, the relative entropy is not a perfect metric because of its asymmetrical property, and using relative entropy as a metric will introduce false positive or false negative.

Researchers also used stochastic methods in the frequency domain and data mining techniques for DDoS detection [24, 25]. Cheng et al. [24] mapped DDoS attacks from the time domain to the frequency domain, and further transformed to the power spectral density to identify DDoS attacks. Lu et al. [25] adopted data mining technology to dig out the DDoS attack information.

Moreover, information theory based methods were also powerful tools for DDoS detection. Sengar et al. [26] used information distance (Hellinger's distance) to detect VoIP floods in peer-to-peer networks. We use the KL-distance for DDoS detection at network layer [27].

3.2   Feature Based Detection Methods

A common methodology for anomaly detection is to identify normal patterns of the study objects, and an action out of the normal patterns is treated as an anomaly. This method has been widely applied in various security detection. We note that this strategy inherits false negative and false positive by its nature.

3.2.1   Profile Based Detection

A common strategy to disguise attack sources is IP spoofing. In order to fight against source IP spoofing, a hop-count filter is an effective method. Wang et al. [2] found that a hacker cannot falsify the number of hops an IP packet takes to reach its destination although he can forge any field in the IP header. Moreover, a receiver can infer the hop-count information based on the Time-to-Live field of the IP header. At the same time, it is easy for a Internet server to establish a table of IP address and their related hop-counts for its legitimate clients, which is called IP-to-hop-count (IP2HC) mapping table. Based on this table, defenders can therefore discriminate spoofed IPs from legitimate IPs.

The authors analyzed the detection rate in three cases: single source, multiple sources, and multiple sources with an awareness of the detection method. We rewrite the analysis by our understanding from the original paper.

In the single source case, suppose the hacker spoofs the IP source address using an IP address of a legitimate client, C_i, of the victim. Moreover, suppose C_i usually submits n_i legitimate packets to the victim for a given time interval. We assume the attacker pumps N_i attack packets to the victim for the same time interval. Obviously,

$N_i \gg n_i$. Among the N_i attack packets, n_i will be treated as legitimate ones. The detection rate is as follows.

$$Z_s = 1 - \frac{n_i}{N_i} = 1 - \alpha_i, \tag{3.1}$$

where α_i is called a *fraction* following the terms of the original paper.

In the $n(n > 1)$ multiple source case, we suppose the hacker uses n legitimate users' IP addresses for spoofing, denoted as $C_1, C_2, \ldots, C_n$, each of them pumps $N_1, N_2, \ldots, N_n$ packets to the victim, and their related fractions are $\alpha_1, \alpha_2, \ldots, \alpha_n$, respectively. We obtain the detection rate as

$$Z_m = \frac{\sum_{i=1}^n (1 - \alpha_i) N_i}{\sum_{i=1}^n N_i}. \tag{3.2}$$

In the case that the spoofed packets are uniformly distributed among the n IP address, we have

$$Z_m = 1 - \frac{1}{n} \sum_{i=1}^n \alpha_i. \tag{3.3}$$

In the third case, if an attacker knows the existence of the detection method, but no further information. One anti-detection strategy he or she may take is to generate initial TTLs with a range of $[h_m, h_n]$ using a given distribution, such as an uniform distribution or a Gaussian distribution. Suppose the probability of hop-count h_k is p_k for the chosen distribution. Following the previous definition, we suppose the fraction of the legitimate IP address that has a hop-count of h_k is α_k, then the detection rate in this case is

$$Z_{anti} = 1 - \sum_{k=m}^n \alpha_k p_k. \tag{3.4}$$

We note that in general if a hacker understands the victim better, he or she can obtain a lower detection rate in the defender's viewpoint.

Packet score [4] is another DDoS detection method at a potential victim end. Suppose we know the statistical distribution of legitimate packets, then based on Bayes inference, we can obtain the probability of its legitimacy of an incoming packet. The basic idea is as follows. Suppose each packet possesses a number of attributes, such as $A, B, \ldots$. Let the value space for the attributes are $\{a_1, a_2, \ldots\}$, $\{b_1, b_2, \ldots\}$, and so on. They use N_a, N_n, and N_m to represent the number of packets for attack packets, normal packets, and measured packets (subscript a, n, and m stand for attack, normal and measured, respectively). For a given time interval, it is straight that

$$N_m = N_a + N_n \tag{3.5}$$

Let function $C()$ be an accounter, and using the same meaning of subscripts a, n, and m, we have

$$N_n = \sum_{k=1}^{\infty} C_n(A = a_k) = \sum_{k=1}^{\infty} C_n(B = b_k) = \ldots \tag{3.6}$$

Similarly,

$$N_a = \sum_{k=1}^{\infty} C_a(A = a_k) = \sum_{k=1}^{\infty} C_a(B = b_k) = \ldots \tag{3.7}$$

$$N_m = \sum_{k=1}^{\infty} C_m(A = a_k) = \sum_{k=1}^{\infty} C_m(B = b_k) = \ldots \tag{3.8}$$

Following these, we obtain the probability distribution for each attribute of a packet in normal, attack and measured cases.

$$Pr_n(A = a_i) = \frac{C_n(A = a_i)}{N_n}, \tag{3.9}$$

$$Pr_n(B = b_i) = \frac{C_n(B = b_i)}{N_n}, \tag{3.10}$$

$$\ldots,$$

where $i = 1, 2, \ldots$.

Likewise, we have $Pr_a(A = a_i), Pr_a(B = b_i), \ldots$, as well as $Pr_m(A = a_i), Pr_m(B = b_i), \ldots$. The joint probability distribution among attributes for normal, attack and measured cases can be calculated by

$$Pr_n(A = a_i, B = b_j, \ldots) = \frac{C_n(A = a_i, B = b_j, \ldots)}{N_n} \tag{3.11}$$

$$Pr_a(A = a_i, B = b_j, \ldots) = \frac{C_n(A = a_i, B = b_j, \ldots)}{N_a} \tag{3.12}$$

$$Pr_m(A = a_i, B = b_j, \ldots) = \frac{C_n(A = a_i, B = b_j, \ldots)}{N_m} \tag{3.13}$$

The authors defined the conditional legitimate probability (CLP) for a packet p as follows.

$$CLP(p) = Pr\{p = legitimate | p.A = a_p, p.B = b_p, \ldots\}, \tag{3.14}$$

where $p.X$ denotes the attribute X of packet p.

With all these parameters in place, we can use the Bayes inference to calculate the packet score (the probability of legitimacy) of packet p as follows.

$$CLP(p) = \frac{Pr\{p = legitimate\} \cap Pr\{A = a_p, B = b_p, \ldots\}}{Pr\{A = a_p, B = b_p, \ldots\}} \qquad (3.15)$$

In order to perform packet discarding, a threshold of $CLP(p)$ is needed, the authors proposed to dynamically adjust the threshold based on the score distribution of recent incoming packets and the current level of system overload.

3.2.2   Low Rate DDoS Attack Detection

Low rate DDoS attack is also called *shrew DDoS attack*, which features with a low attack rate, and it is hard to detect it [28]. Due to the mechanism of low rate DDoS attacks, they inherent a specific characteristic: they submit attack packets periodically. Based on this feature, Chen and Hwang [1] proposed a spectral analysis method to detect this kind of low rate attacks.

The theoretical tools are explained as follows. For a given sequence of network traffic, X, we can denote it as $x[1], x[2], \ldots$. The *autocorrelation* of X is defined as

$$R_{XX}(m) = \frac{1}{N-m} \sum_{n=0}^{N-m+1} x[n]x[n+m]. \qquad (3.16)$$

Autocorrelation function is able to enforcing the periodicity if it exists in the original signal. However, it is still a time domain concept, and is not easy to identify the periodicity. A Discrete Fourier Transform (DFT) of the autocorrelation can clearly display the periodicity in the frequency domain. The definition of DFT is

$$DFT[R_{XX}(m), f] = \frac{1}{N} \sum_{n=0}^{N-1} R_{XX}(m) e^{\frac{-j2\pi fn}{N}}, \qquad (3.17)$$

where $f = 0, 1, \ldots, N-1$.

The output of the DFT processing on autocorrelation is called *power spectrum density* (PSD). We can easily differentiate a shrew DDoS attack from normal network traffic as the PSD of shrew attack is concentrated at the low frequency band, while the PSD of normal traffic is much flatter.

3.3   Network Traffic Based Detection

Network traffic is an important property of the Internet, therefore, it is also a powerful feature for DDoS detection at the network layer. Scherrer et al. investigated Internet traffic patterns thoroughly and proposed the Mean Quadratic Distances to measure traffic anomalies to discriminate DDoS traffic from flash crowds [29]. Lu, Wu et al. transformed the DDoS detection problem into a signal processing problem and then employed data mining technologies to extract DDoS attack information [25]. The wavelets method was applied to complete the task in [30]. Moreover, a wavelets technique developed in [31] was practiced in [32] to observe energy fingerprints to discriminate DDoS attack flows from legitimate flows.

Due to the nature of the anarchy management fashion of the Internet, most of the network traffic based DDoS detections are performed at local area networks. In a local area network, system administrators can manage and configure the routers. As a result, the routers can cooperate with each other to detect possible attacks.

The topology of a local area network can be treated as a graph, however, due to the aggregation feature of DDoS attacks, the attack paths in a local area network form a tree that rooted at the victim. We use Fig. 3.1 as a sample DDoS attack tree in a local area network for our following discussion.

In Fig. 3.1, routers R_6, R_9, R_8 and R_5 are at the edge of the local area network (we call them *edge routers*), and R_0 is the router connected to the victim.

It is necessary to know what is a flow before we progress to any analysis.

Definition 3.3.1. Flow. At a given router in a local area network, all the passing packets that share the same destination address are categorized as one flow.

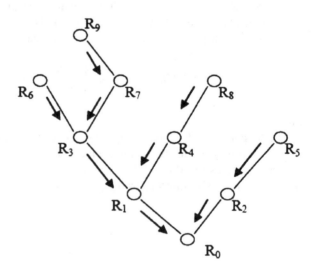

Fig. 3.1 A DDoS attack tree
in a local area network

According to Definition 3.3.1, many flows may coexist at a router in a local area network. In the case of an ongoing DDoS attack, there exists one flow addressed to the victim. We call it *attack flow*. At the same time, there are many other flows that are addressed to different destinations. Different from the source IP addresses or TTL values of the attack packets, the attack flow cannot be spoofed or changed by hackers as the address of the victim is given. Therefore, flow based detection is independent of any specific attack features, and it can deal with new types of flooding attacks.

Once we have flows in place, we need metrics to measure flows for anomaly detection. Entropy is a fundamental metric in information theory [33]. The entropy of a discrete random variable X is defined as

$$H(X) = - \sum_{x \in \chi} \Pr\{X = x\} \log \Pr\{X = x\}, \qquad (3.18)$$

where χ is the sample space of X. The entropy of a random variable X measures the uncertainty of X in the unit of bits.

For our detection purpose, we define flow entropy as follows.

Definition 3.3.2. Flow Entropy. Following Eq. (3.18), the entropy of the flows at a given router is called flow entropy, which represents the randomness of the flows at the router.

In general, the flow entropy of a router is stable in non-DDoS attack cases. However, when a DDoS flooding attack is ongoing, the attack flows will dominate the traffic on local area network routers, and consequently, the flow entropy drops dramatically in a very short time period, such as a few seconds. Therefore, we can raise a DDoS attack alarm when flow entropy decreases significantly in a short time interval.

We make the following assumptions in order for the following discussion to be clearly understood.

- All attack packets for a given attack session come from one botnet. In other words, they are generated by the same attack tools. It is possible that a victim is attacked by different botnets at the same time, however, we only discuss the one botnet case in this chapter.
- The attack packets enter the local area network via a minimum of two edge routers and attack flows merge at the junction routers.
- The whole network system is linear and stable when the DDoS attack is ongoing.

The detection algorithm is running on all routers in the local area network. The routers, especially the edge routers, monitor the network traffic using flow entropy as the metric. In an attack free case, the flow entropy remains in a stable range. Once there is an attack, the flow entropy drops dramatically because there is either one or a number of flows dominating on the routers. As a result, our detection task is to find a suitable threshold, Δ, for the decrease of flow entropy. When the variation of flow entropy is equal or greater than Δ, it is a DDoS attack. We discuss this method as follows.

Suppose in an attack scenario, an attacker uses a random variable X to control the generation speed of attack packets (we call it *attack rate* or *packet rate* of attack flows). For example, using a constant speed to generate the packets, then

$$Pr\{X = C\} = 1, \tag{3.19}$$

where C is a constant.

Increasing the number of packets according to attacking time t, then

$$X = a \cdot t + b, \tag{3.20}$$

where a, b are constants.

Mimicking the network traffic pattern as the Poisson distribution, then

$$Pr\{X = k\} = \frac{\lambda^k e^{-\lambda}}{k!}, \tag{3.21}$$

where $k = 0, 1, \ldots,$ and λ is constant.

We use a random variable X to represent the packet rates of flows on a router within a given time interval. Let vector $X = \{x_1, x_2, \ldots, x_n\}$ denote the number of packets for n flows, respectively. We then have the probability distribution of the flows as

$$p(x_i) = x_i \cdot \left(\sum_{j=1}^{n} x_j \right)^{-1} \tag{3.22}$$

We use $H_f(X)$ to represent the flow entropy of flows on a given router. According to our previous definitions, we have

$$H_f(X) = - \sum_{i=1}^{n} p(x_i) \log p(x_i). \tag{3.23}$$

As discussed previously, $H_f(X)$ is stable in general with minor fluctuations in normal network operations. However, in a DDoS attack scenario, the packet rate of the flow that targets the victim is significantly larger than the packet rates of other legitimate flows at the same router. Therefore, $H_f(x)$ decreases dramatically. Let $\Delta (\Delta > 0)$ be a given real number as the threshold. We can then use the following inequality to identify DDoS flooding attacks.

$$H_f(X) \mid_{t=t_0} - H_f(X) \mid_{t=t_0 + \Delta t} \geq \Delta, \tag{3.24}$$

where t represents time, and $\Delta t (\Delta t > 0)$ represents a short time interval. Our task is to find a suitable threshold Δ.

If $H_f(X)$ is differentiable at t_0, then inequality (3.24) can be further developed to

$$H_f^{'}(X) = \lim_{\Delta t \to 0} \frac{H_f(X)\mid_{t=t_0+\Delta t} - H_f(X)\mid_{t=t_0}}{\Delta t}. \qquad (3.25)$$

Combining inequality (3.24) and Eq. (3.25), we obtain

$$H_f^{'}(X) \leq -\Delta \qquad (3.26)$$

3.4 Detection Against Mimicking Attacks

It is critical for defenders to detect flash crowds mimicking DDoS attacks from genuine flash crowds [1, 22, 34]. If we fail to achieve this, then attackers can mimic the traffic features of flash crowds to disable our detectors; yet on the other hand, our detectors may treat legitimate flash crowds as DDoS attacks (also referred as false positive). The early research on discriminating DDoS attack flows from legitimate flows can be found in [35], however, delay and converging issues are not explored in this work. Jung et al. [34] tried to discriminate flash crowds from DoS attacks using three features: traffic patterns, client characteristics and file reference characteristics. Unfortunately, this counter attack method cannot follow the ever changing methods of attack. Moreover, the attacker will be able to disable the detector easily by mimicking the network traffic patterns of flash crowds. The entropy detector mentioned in the survey [22] came from [14]. Entropy detectors have the capacity to raise alarms of crowd access, however, it has difficulty discriminating DDoS attacks from the surge of legitimate accesses like flash crowds. Cheng and Hwang tried to separate flash crowds from DDoS flooding using the change-point detection method [1].

Human behavior has been employed to discriminate DDoS attacks from flash crowds. Xie and Yu [36, 37] deploy user browsing dynamics to differentiate flash crowds and DDoS attacks. In general, the popularity of web pages for a given web site follows the Zipf distribution, however, the DDoS attack requests do not possess this property. Moreover, user browsing pattern is also used to achieve the goal, e.g. the number of requests from a user for a given time interval. A semi-Markov model based access matrix has been established to carry out the differentiation task. Oikonomou and Mirkovic tried to differentiate the two by modeling human behavior, e.g. request dynamics and request semantics [38].

Based on the available literature, we found the following facts concerning the current botnets.

1. The attack tools are prebuilt programs, which are usually the same for one botnet. A botmaster issues a command to all bots in his botnet to start one attack session.
2. The attack flows that we observe at the victim end are an aggregation of many original attack flows, and the aggregated attack flows share a similar standard

deviation as an original attack flow, and the flow standard deviation is usually smaller than that of genuine flash crowd flows. The reason for this phenomenon is that the number of live bots of a current botnet is far less than the number of concurrent legitimate users of a flash crowd. Rajab et al. [39] recently reported that the live bots of a botnet is at the hundreds or a few thousands level for a given time point. However, we observed that the number of concurrent users of the flash crowds of World Cup 98 is at the hundreds of thousands level. Therefore, in order to launch a flash crowd attack, a botmaster has to force his live bots to generate many more attack packets, e.g., web page requests, than that of a legitimate user.

Based on this observation, we found that the similarity among the current DDoS attack flows is higher than that of a flash crowd. Therefore, we can take advantage of this feature to discriminate DDoS attacks from flash crowds.

3.4.1   Similarity Metrics

Similarity or distance measurement has been explored extensively for many years. Researchers have invented many metrics for similarity measurement, which includes first order and second order metrics. For example, mean and the Kullback-Leibler distance are first order metrics, while standard deviation and correntropy [40] are second order metrics. Of course, there are many different metrics for different purposes and applications, we discuss only a few of them here for our detection purpose.

For two given flows or sequence P and Q, we denote their probability distribution as $p(x)$ and $q(x)$, respectively. In order to measure the distance or similarity between them, we need metrics.

A frequently used distance metric is the *Kullback-Leibler distance* (KL distance in short), which is defined as

$$D(p,q) = \sum_{x \in \chi} p(x) \cdot \log \frac{p(x)}{q(x)}, \qquad (3.27)$$

where χ is the sample space of x. It is obvious that $D(p,q) \neq D(q,p)$, if $p \neq q$. As a result, the KL distance is not a metric in a rigorous sense, although it has been widely used in practice.

Jeffrey distance fixes this asymmetric using combination of the Kullback-Leibler distance, which is defined as follows.

$$D_J(p,q) = \frac{1}{2} [D(p,q) + D(q,p)]. \qquad (3.28)$$

A third metric in this category is the *Sibson distance*, which is defined as

$$D_S(p,q) = \frac{1}{2} \left\{ D\left(p, \frac{1}{2}(p+q)\right) + D\left(q, \frac{1}{2}(p+q)\right) \right\}. \qquad (3.29)$$

Different from previous KL distance based metrics, the *Hellinger's distance* is defined as follows.

$$D_H(p,q) = \left[\sum_{x \in \chi} \left(\sqrt{p(x)} - \sqrt{q(x)} \right)^2 \right]^{\frac{1}{2}}. \qquad (3.30)$$

All the metrics that we have seen can be categorized as first order metrics. Our previous study [41] indicates that the Sibson distance is the best metric among these first order metrics for DDoS attack detection purpose.

In the following we discuss two second order metrics. The first one is *correlation*, which is a widely used in engineering.

Let X_i and X_j $(i \neq j)$ be two flows with the same length N, then the correlation between the two flows is defined as

$$r_{X_i,X_j} = \frac{1}{N} \sum_{n=1}^{N} x_i[n] x_j[n]. \qquad (3.31)$$

The correlation is used to describe the similarity of different flows. However, in some cases, it may indicate zero correlation although the two flows are completely correlated but with a phase difference. Therefore, the definition is modified to be practical as follows.

$$r_{X_i,X_j}[k] = \frac{1}{N} \sum_{n=1}^{N} x_i[n] x_j[n+k], \qquad (3.32)$$

where $k(k = 0, 1, 2, \ldots, N-1)$ is the position shift of flow X_j.

However, there might still be a magnitude difference for the same similarity in different scenarios, therefore, unification is necessary. We define the correlation coefficient of the two flows as

$$\rho_{X_i,X_j}[k] = \frac{r_{X_i,X_j}[k]}{\frac{1}{N} \left[\sum_{n=1}^{N-1} x_i^2[n] \sum_{n=1}^{N-1} x_j^2[n] \right]^{1/2}}. \qquad (3.33)$$

Correlation coefficient has been used as a similarity metric for various network flow applications. For example, fast similarity search for video sequence on the web [42], distance learning on images [43], and similarity measurement among VoIP flows [26]. We noticed that abstract distance does not include time information, and it is sensitive to fluctuation of flows. However, the correlation coefficient is better than abstract distances in terms of stability. There are also some variants of correlation coefficient as metrics for similarity, such as order statistics correlation coefficient [44]. This method sorts the original items of sequence and, as a result, the timing information of the original signal will be lost, it is similar to the spectrum methodology.

Fig. 3.2 A sample
community network with
flows

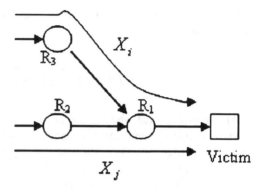

The next second order metric we discuss is correntropy, which is a recently
invented local tool for second-order similarity measurement in statistics. It works
independently on measuring pair-wise arbitrary samples. Correntropy features sym-
metric, positive, and bounded under a clear theoretical foundation.

For any two finite data sequences A and B, suppose we have sample
$\{(A_j, B_j)\}_{j=1}^m, m \in \mathbb{N}$, then the similarity of the sequences are estimated as

$$\hat{V}_{m,\sigma}(A,B) = \frac{1}{m} \sum_{j=1}^{m} k_\sigma(A_j - B_j), \qquad (3.34)$$

where $k_\sigma(\cdot)$ is the Gaussian kernel, which is usually defined as

$$g(x) \triangleq exp(-\frac{x^2}{2\sigma^2}). \qquad (3.35)$$

Correntropy is widely used in various disciplines, such as face recognition [45].

3.4.2 Flow Correlation Based Discrimination

Most of the detections are conducted at the potential victim end, which we usually
also call it *community network*

A sample community network with flows is shown in Fig. 3.2. In the sample
community network, R_2 and R_3 are the edge routers, and the server is a potential
victim that we try to protect. There are two incoming flows, X_i and X_j. They merge
at router R_1 and both are addressed to the potential victim, and enter the community
network via different paths. We sample the number of packets for a given network
flow with a given time interval. Therefore, a network flow can also be represented
by a data sequence $X_i[n]$, where $i(i \geq 1)$ is the index of network flows, and n denotes

the nth element in the data sequence. For example, if the length of a given network flow X_i is N, then the network flow can be presented as follows.

$$X_i[n] = \{x_i[1], x_i[2], \cdots, x_i[N]\}, \qquad (3.36)$$

where $x_i[k]\,(1 \leq k \leq N)$ represents the number of packets that we counted in the kth time interval for the network flow. According to our definition of flow, a router may have many network flows at any given point of time.

Definition 3.4.1. Flow strength. For a network flow X_i, let the length of the network flow be $N(N \geqslant 1)$. We define the expectation of the data sequence as the flow strength of X_i as follows.

Flow strength represents the average packet rate of a network flow. If X_i is a DDoS attack flow, then we call $E[X_i]$ attack strength.

$$E[X_i] = \frac{1}{N} \sum_{n=1}^{N} x_i[n] \qquad (3.37)$$

Definition 3.4.2. Fingerprint of flow. For a given network flow X_i with length N, its fingerprint X_i' is the unified representation of X_i, namely

$$\begin{aligned} X_i' &= \left\{ x_i'[1], x_i'[2], \ldots, x_i'[N] \right\} \\ &= \left\{ \frac{x_i[1]}{N \cdot E[X_i]}, \frac{x_i[2]}{N \cdot E[X_i]}, \cdots, \frac{x_i[N]}{N \cdot E[X_i]} \right\} \end{aligned} \qquad (3.38)$$

Following this definition, we know $\sum_{k=1}^{N} x_i'[k] = 1$. We can see that fingerprint of flow is essentially an instance of its probability density distribution.

Based on Eqs. (3.37) and (3.38), we obtained the following relationship between a network flow and its fingerprint.

$$X_i = N \cdot E[X_i] \cdot X_i' \qquad (3.39)$$

As previously discussed, the current botnets, such as SDbot, Rbot and Spybot, employ the same program to generate attack packets. Furthermore, they try to create as many attack packets as they can, usually with a very short delay (1 or 5 ms) between two attack packets. This confirms that flow fingerprint does exist in attack flows for a given botnet.

We set up an overlay network on the routers in the community network that we have control over. We execute software on every router to count the number of packets for every flow and record this information for a short period of time at every router. Once an attack alarm goes off, the similarity among different suspected flows will be calculated, and a decision on whether it is a DDoS attack or flash crowd will be made based on the global information of the community network. Under this framework, the requirement of storage space is very limited and an online decision can be achieved.

A real community network may be much complex with more routers and servers than the sample network in Fig. 3.2. However, for a given server, we can always treat the related community network as a tree, which is rooted at the server. We must point out that the topology of the community network has no impact on our detection strategy, whether it is a graph or a tree, because our detection method based on flow rather than network topology.

Once a surge on the server occurs, our task is to identify whether it is a genuine flash crowds or a DDoS attack. As we just discussed, when a possible DDoS attack alarm goes off, the routers in the community network start to sample the suspected flows by counting the number of packets for a given time interval, for example, 100 ms. When the length of a flow, N, is sufficient, we start to calculate flow correlation coefficient among suspected flows. We discriminate DDoS attacks from flash crowds based on the aforementioned fact: in DDoS attacks, the suspicious network flows have a strong correlation although they are a mixture of a number of original attack flows with different delays. On the other hand, flow correlation coefficient among two flash crowds is weaker compared to that of two attack flows.

Suppose we have sampled M network flows, $X_1, X_2, \ldots, X_M$, therefore, we can obtain the flow correlation coefficient of any two network flows, $X_i (1 \leq i \leq M)$ and $X_j (1 \leq j \leq M, i \neq j)$. Let I_{X_i,X_j} be the indication function for flow X_i and X_j, and I_{X_i,X_j} has only two possible values: 1 for DDoS attacks and 0 otherwise. Let δ be the threshold for the discrimination, then we have

$$I_{X_i,X_j} = \begin{cases} 1, \ \rho_{X_i,X_j}[k] \geq \delta \\ \\ 0, \ otherwise, \end{cases} \tag{3.40}$$

where $1 \leq i, j \leq M$, and $i \neq j$.

In general, we may have more than two suspected flows in a community network. This means we can conduct a number of different pairwise comparisons, and the final decision can be derived from them in order to improve the reliability of our decision.

3.4.3   System Analysis on the Discrimination Method

In this section, we first present the difference between a flash crowd traffic and a DDoS attack traffic, and then we prove that the two can be discriminated using flow correlation coefficient. Following this foundation, we theoretically analyze the effectiveness of the proposed discrimination method, and prove that the threshold δ in Eq. (3.40) does exist. We then explore the relationship between flow correlation coefficient and the length of flows. These pave the way for the implementation of the proposed method in practice. The attack flow converging issue is also addressed in this section.

In order to make our analysis clear, we make the following assumptions.

1. There is only one server in a community network which is under attack or experiencing flash crowds at any given time.
2. The attack packets enter the community network via a minimum of two different edge routers.
3. In one attack session, all the attack packets are generated by only one botnet, therefore the fingerprints of the attack flows are the same.
4. The network delays are discrete and countable.

First of all, we investigate the difference between a DDoS attack and a flash crowds in terms of traffic distribution. We suppose there is a flash crowd, and the statistics is known to everyone (including attackers), say the mean $n\mu$. Moreover, the botmaster has n alive bots to execute flash crowd attack. As we know from the previous research [46], the number of living bots is usually at hundreds or thousands level, however, the number of users to generate a flash crowds is quite big. For example, 360,000 browsers at the same time. As a result, botmaster must exhaust all living bots to generate attack traffic as many as they can, and in average the mean has to be as much as μ for a bot. For this reason, the timer interval of the attack packets should be as small as possible in order to pump sufficient attacking packets. This results in the standard variation of packet arrivals very small, for example $\sigma = 0.01\mu$ ($\sigma = 0$ is the best from hackers viewpoint). All the attack traffic aggregated and measured at the victim's location. Although the aggregated attack traffic obtains the mean of the flash crowd, $n\mu$, however, the its standard variation is bounded in a narrow space, e.g., 0.01μ. On the other hand, the flash crowd traffic is created by many users, it is a genuine distribution, the standard variation is much lager than that of the attack traffic.

We make an example to explain this as shown in Fig. 3.3. The aggregated traffic came from 50 Gaussian distributions, with $\mu = 10$ and $\sigma = 0.01\mu = 0.1$ for each bot; the single distribution is a Gaussian distribution with $\mu' = 50$ and $\sigma' = 0.01\mu' = 0.5$. We can find the difference from the figure as we discussed.

Following this observation, we will theoretically prove that the DDoS attack traffic and flash crowd traffic can be differentiated using flow correlation coefficient as a metric.

Theorem 3.4.1. *Let X_i and X_j $(i \neq j)$ be two traffic flows that share the same distribution, and the standard variation is σ is a random variable, the correlation coefficient of the two flows is inverse proportional to σ, namely, $\rho_{X_i,X_j} \propto \frac{1}{\sigma}$.*

Proof. Let f_i and f_j be the mathematical functions to generate X_i and X_j, respectively. Let random variable μ be the mean of the distribution, and another random variable σ represent the standard variation, and we know that the mean of σ is 0. Without loss of generality, let

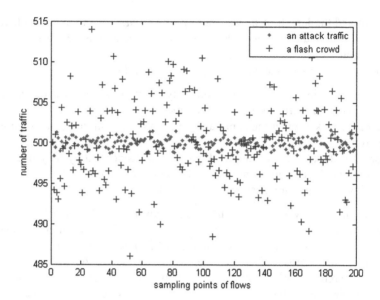

Fig. 3.3 The difference between an aggregated attack traffic and a flash crowd traffic

$$\begin{cases} f_i = u + \sigma \\ f_j = u - \sigma \end{cases}$$

As X_i and X_j possess the same mean, μ, and there is no phase issue for the two flows. Therefore, we can simply use Eq. (3.31). Suppose we have N samples in X_i and X_j, respectively. We have

$$\begin{cases} X_i = \{u_1 + \sigma, u_2 + \sigma, \dots, u_N + \sigma\} \\ X_j = \{u_1 - \sigma, u_2 - \sigma, \dots, u_N - \sigma\} \end{cases}$$

Therefore,

$$\rho_{X_i, X_j} = r_{X_i, X_j} = \frac{1}{N} \sum_{i=1}^{N} (u_i^2 - \sigma^2) \approx \overline{u}^2 - \sigma^2,$$

where $\overline{\mu}$ is the mean of the random variable μ. Once $\overline{\mu}$ is given, a larger standard variation σ results a lower correlation coefficient among the flows, and vice vasa.

Based on Theorem 3.4.1, it is true that we can differentiate DDoS attack flows from flash crowds as the standard variations between these two phenomenons are different. We have to bear in mind that Theorem 3.4.1 is proved in a circumstance of no background noise case.

We now investigate the flow correlation coefficient of any two independent network flows, such as flash crowd flows. Previous research has demonstrated that the web traffic follows the Pareto law [47, 48], hence, the Pareto distribution represents the flow fingerprint of flash crowds. The definition of the distribution is as follows.

Let X be a random variable, and x_m be the minimum time interval for arrival packets. For a given arrival time interval x, the probability density function of the Pareto distribution is given by

$$Pr\{X = x\} = \alpha \cdot x_m^{\alpha} \cdot x^{-(\alpha+1)}, \tag{3.41}$$

where $x_m \leq x$, and α is the *Pareto index*.

Theorem 3.4.2. *Given two identical independent flash crowd flow X_i and X_j $(i \neq j)$ with same length N, we have $\lim_{N \to \infty} \rho_{X_i, X_j}[k] = 0$.*

Proof. As flash crowds, X_i and X_j follow Eq. (3.41). Let t be the index for both X_i and X_j. The probability of $x_i[t] = x_j[t] = x$ is

$$Pr\{x_i[t] = x_j[t] = x\} = \left[\frac{\alpha \cdot x_m^{\alpha}}{x^{(\alpha+1)}}\right]^2 < 1 \tag{3.42}$$

If $X_i = X_j$, namely $x_i[t] = x_j[t]$ for all $t(1 \leq t \leq N)$, then the probability is

$$\begin{aligned} Pr\{X_i = X_j\} &= \left[Pr\{x_i[t] = x_j[t] = x\}\right]^N \\ &= \left[\frac{\alpha \cdot x_m^{\alpha}}{x^{(\alpha+1)}}\right]^{2N} \end{aligned} \tag{3.43}$$

Based on (3.42) and (3.43), we obtain

$$\lim_{N \to \infty} \rho_{X_i, X_j}[k] = \lim_{N \to \infty} Pr\{X_i = X_j\} = 0$$

Theorem 3.4.2 shows that for any two independent flash crowd flows with length N, the flow correlation coefficient approaches 0 when N approaches infinity.

We can easily obtain the following corollary by extending Theorem 3.4.2.

Corollary 3.4.1. *For two independent flash crowd flow X_i and X_j with same length N, $\forall \delta(\delta < 1)$, $\exists N'$, when $N > N'$, $\rho_{X_i, X_j}[k] < \delta$.*

We now move to explore the flow correlation coefficient among DDoS attack flows. Let us first find the expression of a DDoS attack flow, X_i, which we obtained at an edge router. Suppose the observed attack flow is a mixture of attack flows that came from K different bots, and let X_0' represent the fingerprint of the attack flows. Based on the aforementioned discussion, the fingerprint of different attack flows in one attack session is the same, except that there are delays in different attack flows. Let $X_0'[j]$ represent the fingerprint that is delayed j time units. As a result, the observed attack flow can be denoted as follows.

$$X_i = \Sigma_{j=0}^{K} N \cdot E[X_i] \cdot X_0'[j]$$
$$= \Sigma_{j=0}^{k'} a_j \cdot X_0'[j], \tag{3.44}$$

where $a_j (1 \le j \le k' \le K)$ represents the magnitude of the attack flows that possess the same delay j at the edge router.

Theorem 3.4.3. *Let X_0' be the fingerprint of attack flows for one attack session. Under the condition of no network delay and no background noise, for two mixed attack flows X_i and X_j ($i \ne j$) that we observed at two edge routers, the correlation coefficient of X_i and X_j is 1, namely, $\rho_{X_i,X_j}[k] = 1$.*

Proof. Under the delay free and noise free condition, based on Eq. (3.44), we can write X_i and X_j as follows.

$$\begin{cases} X_i = \Sigma_{p=0}^{k_1} a_p \cdot X_0' \\[2em] X_j = \Sigma_{q=0}^{k_2} a_q \cdot X_0' \end{cases}$$

Let victor $B_i = (a_{11}, a_{12}, \ldots a_{1k_1})'$, $B_j = (a_{21}, a_{22}, \ldots a_{2k_2})'$ and $k = \max(k_1, k_2)$, We try to make the length of B_i and B_j equivalent by filling zeroes to the shorter one. We then obtain $A_i = (a_{11}, a_{12}, \ldots a_{1k})$ and $A_j = (a_{21}, a_{22}, \ldots a_{2k})$ from B_i and B_j, respectively. Following these, we can rewrite X_i and X_j as follows.

$$\begin{cases} X_i = X_0' \cdot A_i \\[2em] X_j = X_0' \cdot A_j, \end{cases}$$

where A_i and A_j are the mixture matrix for different merging of the attack flows, respectively.

As we can always shift one flow to match the other to make them synchronized. Based on Eq. (3.32), we obtain

$$r_{X_i,X_j}[j] = \frac{1}{N} \sum_{n=1}^{N} x_i[n] x_j[n+j]$$

$$= \frac{1}{N} \sum_{n=1}^{N} x_i[n] x_j[n] = \frac{1}{N} (A_j' \cdot A_i) \left(X_0'[n] \right)^2 \tag{3.45}$$

Combining Eq. (3.45) with Eq. (3.33), we obtain

$$\rho_{X_i,X_j}[k] = \frac{r_{X_i,X_j}[k]}{\frac{1}{N}\left[\sum_{n=1}^{N} x_i^2[n] \sum_{n=1}^{N} x_j^2[n]\right]^{1/2}}$$

$$= \frac{r_{X_i,X_j}[k]}{\frac{1}{N}\left[(A_i'A_i)\left(X_0'[n]\right)^2 \cdot (A_j'A_j)\left(X_0'[n]\right)^2\right]^{1/2}} \qquad (3.46)$$

Because $A_i' \cdot A_j = A_j' \cdot A_i$, and substitute this in Eq. (3.46), we have

$$\rho_{X_i,X_j}[k] = \frac{r_{X_i,X_j}[k]}{\frac{1}{N}\left[(A_j'A_i)^2 \left(X_0'[n]\right)^4\right]^{1/2}} = 1$$

Theorem 3.4.3 demonstrates that in an ideal condition of delay and noise free environment, any two DDoS attack flows from one botnet are totally correlated because they are a combination of attack flows from different bots with different routes.

In reality, however, delay and noise do exist and bots in a centralized botnet are coordinated by their botmaster. This means the delays among the attack flows from different bots depend on normal Internet delays, and therefore is limited when compared with fast Internet transportation facilities. As a result, the delay free condition can be satisfied to some degree. On the other hand, noise in attack flows are the legitimate packets that are also addressed to the victim at the same time as a DDoS attack is ongoing. However, the strength of the noise is much smaller compared with the strength of DDoS flooding attack flows.

Following Theorem 3.4.3, we can further have the following corollary.

Corollary 3.4.2. *Let Y_i and Y_j be the noises for two DDoS attack flows X_i and X_j from one attack session, $\forall \delta(\delta < 1)$, $\exists \Delta$, $\rho_{X_i,X_j}[k] \geq \delta$ holds when $\frac{E[X_i]}{E[Y_i]} > \Delta$ and $\frac{E[X_j]}{E[Y_j]} > \Delta$.*

Proof. From Theorem 3.4.3, we know that $\rho_{X_i,X_j}[k] = 1$ when $E[Y_i] = E[Y_j] = 0$; On the other hand, if the strength of noise is much stronger than that of signal, namely, $E[Y_i] \gg E[X_i]$ and $E[Y_j] \gg E[X_j]$, then

$$\begin{cases} Y_i \approx Y_i + X_i \\ \\ Y_j \approx Y_j + X_j \end{cases}$$

As a result, $\rho_{X_i+Y_i,X_j+Y_j}[k] \approx \rho_{Y_i,Y_j}[k]$. Based on Theorem 3.4.2, we know $\rho_{Y_i,Y_j}[k] \rightarrow 0$ when the length N increases, namely, $\rho_{X_i,X_j}[k] \rightarrow 0$ when N is sufficiently large.

Corollary 3.4.2 indicates that the correlation coefficient of DDoS attack flows approaches 1 if the signal-noise-ratio (SNR), $\frac{E[X_i]}{E[Y_i]}$, is sufficiently large. It is true that $E[X_i] \gg E[Y_i]$ and $E[X_j] \gg E[Y_j]$ for the DDoS flooding attack cases, therefore, the correlation coefficient of attack flows is close to 1 in an ongoing DDoS attack scenario.

Theorem 3.4.4. *DDoS attack flow can be discriminated from flash crowds by flow correlation coefficient at edge routers under two conditions: the length of the sampled flow is sufficiently large, and the DDoS flooding attack strength is sufficiently strong.*

Proof. Let X_i and X_j ($i \neq j$) be two random flash crowds, X_p and X_q ($p \neq q$) be two DDoS flooding attack flows, and let $\delta(\delta < 1)$ be a given small real number. Based on Corollary 3.4.1, the following equation holds with condition on N.

$$Pr\{\rho_{X_i,X_j}[k] < \delta | N\} = 1 \tag{3.47}$$

From Theorem 3.4.2, we are sure that the following equation holds as well with condition on N and signal-noise-rate (SNR).

$$Pr\{\rho_{X_p,X_q}[k] \geq \delta | N, SNR\} = 1 \tag{3.48}$$

We know that $\rho_{X_i,X_j}[k]$ is a decrease function on the length of flow, N; $\rho_{X_p,X_q}[k] = 1$ when there is no noise and no delay, and it decreases when the strength of noise increases, therefore, there must exist a point where both Eq. (3.47) and (3.48) hold, and Theorem 3.4.3 holds as well.

It is practical that we obtain a upper bounds, δ, of flow correlation coefficient for flash crowds for a given flow length. In a case that flow correlation coefficient is greater than δ, then they are DDoS attack flows.

In a DDoS attack or flash crowds, we usually can have a number of suspected flows. Suppose we have maximum M suspected flows, from which we calculate the flow correlation coefficient I_{X_i,X_j} for any two different flows X_i and X_j($1 \leq i, j \leq M, i \neq j$). We can therefore have an integrated DDoS attack positive probability as follows.

$$Pr\{I_A = 1\} = \frac{\sum_{1 \leq i,j \leq M, i \neq j} I_{X_i,X_j}}{\binom{M}{2}}, \tag{3.49}$$

where I_A is the indicator for DDoS attacks, and $I_A = 1$ represents positive for DDoS attacks. We make our final decision with global information as follows.

$$I_A = \begin{cases} 1 \; , \; Pr\{I_A = 1\} \geq 0.5 \\\\ 0 \; , \; Pr\{I_A = 1\} < 0.5 \end{cases} \tag{3.50}$$

In other words, it is a DDoS attack if at least half of the comparisons are positive; Otherwise, it is not DDoS attack.

References

1. Y. Chen and K. Hwang, "Collaborative detection and filtering of shrew ddos attacks using spectral analysis," *Journal of Parallel Distributed Computing*, vol. 66, no. 9, pp. 1137–1151, 2006.
2. H. Wang, C. Jin, and K. G. Shin, "Defense against spoofed ip traffic using hop-count filtering," *IEEE/ACM Transactions on Networking*, vol. 15, no. 1, pp. 40–53, 2007.
3. B. Al-Duwairi and G. Manimaran, "Novel hybrid schemes employing packet marking and logging for ip traceback," *IEEE Transactions on Parallel and Distributed Systems*, vol. 17, no. 5, pp. 403–418, 2006.
4. Y. Kim, W. C. Lau, M. C. Chuah, and H. J. Chao, "Packetscore: A statistics-based packet filtering scheme against distributed denial-of-service attacks," *IEEE Transactions on Dependable and Secure Computing*, vol. 3, no. 2, pp. 141–155, 2006.
5. R. R. Kompella, S. Singh, and G. Varghese, "On scalable attack detection in the network," *IEEE/ACM Transactions on Networking*, vol. 15, no. 1, pp. 14–25, 2007.
6. P. E. Ayres, H. Sun, H. J. Chao, and W. C. Lau, "Alpi: A ddos defense system for high-speed networks," *IEEE Journal on Selected Areas in Communications*, vol. 24, no. 10, pp. 1864–1876, 2006.
7. Y. Xiong, S. Liu, and P. Sun, "On the defense of the distributed denial of service attacks: an on-off feedback control approach," *IEEE Transactions on Systems, Man, and Cybernetics, Part A*, vol. 31, no. 4, pp. 282–293, 2001.
8. R. Chen, J.-M. Park, and R. Marchany, "A divide-and-conquer strategy for thwarting distributed denial-of-service attacks," *IEEE Transactions on Parallel and Distributed Systems*, vol. 18, no. 5, pp. 577–588, 2007.
9. A. Yaar, A. Perrig, and D. Song, "Stackpi: New packet marking and filtering mechanisms for ddos and ip spoofing defense," *IEEE Journal on Selected Areas in Communications*, vol. 24, no. 10, pp. 1853–1863, 2006.
10. A. Bremler-Barr and H. Levy, "Spoofing prevention method," in *Proceedings of INFOCOM*, 2005, pp. 536–547.
11. H. Aljifri, "Ip traceback: A new denial-of-service deterrent?" *IEEE Security and Privacy*, vol. 1, pp. 24–31, 2003.
12. A. Yaar, A. Perrig, and D. X. Song, "Fit: fast internet traceback," in *Proceedings of the INFOCOM*, 2005, pp. 1395–1406.
13. M. Sung, J. Xu, J. Li, and L. Li, "Large-scale ip traceback in high-speed internet: practical techniques and information-theoretic foundation," *IEEE/ACM Transactions on Networking*, vol. 16, no. 6, pp. 1253–1266, 2008.
14. L. Feinstein and D. Schnackenberg, "Statistical approaches to ddos attack detection and response," in *Proceedings of the DARPA Information Survivability Conference and Exposition*, 2003, pp. 303–314.
15. D. Moore, C. Shannon, D. J. Brown, G. M. Voelker, and S. Savage, "Inferring internet denial-of-service activity," *ACM Transactions on Computer Systems*, vol. 24, no. 2, pp. 115–139, 2006.

16. A. El-Atawy, E. Al-Shaer, T. Tran, and R. Boutaba, "Adaptive early packet filtering for defending firewalls against dos attacks," in *Proceedings of INFOCOM*, 2009, pp. 2437–2445.

17. F. Soldo, A. Markopoulou, and K. J. Argyraki, "Optimal filtering of source address prefixes: Models and algorithms," in *Proceedings of INFOCOM*, 2009, pp. 2446–2454.

18. P. Barford, J. Kline, D. Plonka, and A. Ron, "A signal analysis of network traffic anomalies," in *Proceedings of the Internet Measurement Workshop*, 2002, pp. 71–82.

19. J. Tang and Y. Cheng, "Quick detection of stealthy sip flooding attacks in voip networks," in *Proceedings of the IEEE ICC*, 2011, pp. 1–5.

20. Z. Duan, X. Yuan, and J. Chandrashekar, "Controlling ip spoofing through interdomain packet filters," *IEEE Transactions on Dependable and Secure Computing*, vol. 5, no. 1, pp. 22–36, 2008.

21. F. Yi, S. Yu, W. Zhou, J. Hai, and A. Bonti, "Source-based filtering algorithm against ddos attacks," *International Journal of Database Theory and Application*, vol. 1, no. 1, pp. 9–20, 2008.

22. G. Carl, G. Kesidis, R. Brooks, and S. Rai, "Denial-of-service attack-detection techniques," *IEEE Internet Computing*, vol. 10, no. 1, pp. 82–89, 2006.

23. W. Lee and D. Xiang, "Information-theoretic measures for anomaly detection," in *Proceedings of the IEEE Symposium on Security and Privacy*, 2001, pp. 130–143.

24. C. Cheng, H. T. Kung, and K. S. Tan, "Use of spectral analysis in defense against dos attacks," in *Proceedings of the IEEE Global Communications Conference*, 2002, pp. 2143–2148.

25. K. Lu, D. Wu, J. Fan, S. Todorovic, and A. Nucci, "Robust and efficient detection of ddos attacks for large-scale internet," *Computer Networks*, vol. 51, no. 9, pp. 5036–5056, 2007.

26. H. Sengar, H. Wang, D. Wijesekera, and S. Jajodia, "Detecting voip floods using the hellinger distance," *IEEE Transactions on Parallel and Distributed Systems*, vol. 19, no. 6, pp. 794–805, 2008.

27. S. Yu, W. Zhou, and R. Doss, "Information theory based detection against network behavior mimicking ddos attack," *IEEE Communications Letters*, vol. 12, no. 4, pp. 319–321, 2008.

28. A. Kuzmanovic and E. W. Knightly, "Low-rate tcp-targeted denial of service attacks: the shrew vs. the mice and elephants," in *Proceedings of the SIGCOMM*, 2003, pp. 75–86.

29. A. Scherrer, N. Larrieu, P. Owezarski, P. Borgnat, and P. Abry, "Non-gaussian and long memory statistical characterizations for internet traffic with anomalies," *IEEE Transactions on Dependable Secure Computing*, vol. 4, no. 1, pp. 56–70, 2007.

30. J. Yuan and K. Miles, "Ddos attack detection and wavelets," National Institute of Standards and Technology, Tech. Rep., 2004.

31. D. Veitch and P. Abry, "A wavelet-based joint estimator of the parameters of long-range dependence," *IEEE Transactions on Information Theory*, vol. 45, no. 3, pp. 878–897, 1999.

32. L. Li and G. Lee, "Ddos attack detection and wavelets," in *Proceedings of the International Conference on Computer Communications and Networks*, 2003.

33. T. M. Cover and J. A. Thomas, *Elements of Information Theory*. John Wiley & Sons, 2006.

34. J. Jung, B. Krishnamurthy, and M. Rabinovich, "Flash crowds and denial of service attacks: Characterization and implications for cdns and web sites," in *Proceedings of the WWW*. IEEE, 2002, pp. 252–262.

35. S. Jin and D. Yeung, "A covariance analysis model for ddos attack detection," in *Proceedings of the INFOCOM*, 2004, pp. 1882–1886.

36. Y. Xie and S.-Z. Yu, "A large-scale hidden semi-markov model for anomaly detection on user browsing behaviors," *IEEE/ACM Transactions on Networking*, vol. 17, no. 1, pp. 54–65, 2009.

37. ——, "Monitoring the application-layer ddos attacks for popular websites," *IEEE/ACM Transactions on Networking*, vol. 17, no. 1, pp. 15–25, 2009.

38. G. Oikonomou and J. Mirkovic, "Modeling human behavior for defense against flash-crowd attacks," in *Proceedings of the INFOCOM*, 2009.

39. M. A. Rajab, J. Zarfoss, F. Monrose, and A. Terzis, "My botnet is bigger than yours (maybe, better than yours): why size estimates remain challenging," in *Proceedings of the first conference on First Workshop on Hot Topics in Understanding Botnets*. USENIX Association, 2007.

40. W. Liu, P. P. Pokharel, and J. C. Principe, "Correntropy: Properties and applications in non-gaussian signal processing," *IEEE Transactions on Signal Processing*, vol. 55, no. 11, pp. 5286–5298, 2007.

41. S. Yu, T. Thapngam, J. Liu, S. Wei, and W. Zhou, "Discriminating ddos flows from flash crowds using information distance," in *Proceedings of the NSS*, 2009, pp. 351–356.

42. S.-C. S. Cheung and A. Zakhor, "Fast similarity search and clustering of video sequences on the world-wide-web," *IEEE Transactions on Multimedia*, vol. 7, no. 3, pp. 524–537, 2005.

43. J. Yu, J. Amores, N. Sebe, P. Radeva, and Q. Tian, "Distance learning for similarity estimation," *IEEE Transactions on Pattern Analysis and Machine Intelligence*, vol. 30, no. 3, pp. 451–462, 2008.

44. W. Xu, C. Chang, Y. S. Hung, S. K. Kwan, and P. C. W. Fung, "Order statistics correlation coefficient as a novel association measurement with applications to biosignal analysis," *IEEE Transactions on Signal Processing*, vol. 55, no. 12, pp. 5552–5563, 2007.

45. R. He, W.-S. Zheng, and B.-G. Hu, "Maximum correntropy criterion for robust face recognition," *IEEE Transactions on Pattern Analysis and Machine Intellegence*, vol. 33, no. 8, pp. 1561–1576, 2011.

46. M. A. Rajab, J. Zarfoss, F. Monrose, and A. Terzis, "My botnet is bigger than yours (maybe, better than yours): why size estimates remain challenging," in *Proceedings of the first conference on Hot Topics in Understanding Botnets*, 2007.

47. V. Paxson and S. Floyd, "Wide area traffic: the failure of poisson modeling," *IEEE/ACM Transactions on Networking*, vol. 3, no. 3, pp. 226–244, 1995.

48. M. E. Crovella and A. Bestavros, "Self-similarity in world wide web traffic: evidence and possible causes," *IEEE/ACM Transactions on Networking*, vol. 5, no. 6, pp. 835–846, 1997.

Chapter 4
Attack Source Traceback

Abstract In this chapter, we investigate the attack source traceback in DDoS defence. We summarize the three major traceback methods to date: probabilistic packet marking, deterministic packet marking and network traffic based traceback methods. We formulate each traceback method, and present analysis for them, respectively.

4.1 Introduction

In cyber security, it is important to find out the attack sources, which is known as *IP traceback* or *traceback*. It is an open and challenging problem for the cyber security community. As most of DDoS attacks are carried out by botnets, we therefore refer attack sources to bots. It is ideal that we can identify the bots in an attack case, such as identifying the IP addresses of the attacking bots. However, it is extremely hard to achieve this at the moment.

The current definition of IP traceback is identifying the closest routers or gateways to the real sources of attack packets.

In order to make the following discussion going smoothly, we firstly clarify the definitions and terms that we use in IP traceback.

As shown in Fig. 4.1, researchers usually treat a DDoS attack diagram as a tree T, which is rooted at the victim, V. The attack sources (bots) locate in LANs behind routers or gateways, we define those initial routers or gateways as the *leaf nodes*, which is denoted as a set L. From L to V, it forms an *attack path* P, including the intermediate routers. Based on the current definition of IP traceback, we need to identify the nodes on the attack tree as far as possible, ideally the nodes in set L.

Due to the memoryless feature of the Internet and the easiness of source IP spoofing in attack packets, a victim cannot identify the source and attack path of an attack packet. As a result, all the traceback schemes need the participation of Internet routers. However, some routers may or may not participate in the traceback process. For example in Fig. 4.1, on the attack path $R_1 - R_2 - R_3 - R_4$, router R_2 and

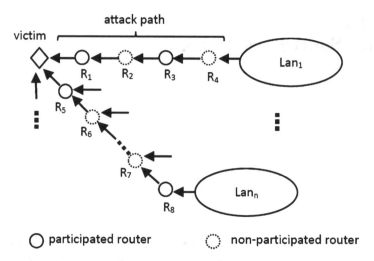

Fig. 4.1 A DDoS attack diagram in the internet environment

R_4 are non-participated routers, therefore, we can at most traceback to R_3 although R_4 is the leaf node. On the other attack path $R_5 - R_6 - R_7 - R_8$, we can possibly trace to the leaf node R_8 although there are some non-participated routers on the attack path.

The current IP traceback methods can be categorized into two classes: packet marking mechanism and network traffic based mechanism. The early work on IP traceback deploy packet marking. In the IPv4 packet head, there are some unused bits, which are usually 17, 19 or 24 bits for different underlay protocols [1]. Network operators can embed special marks or IDs in these available space for traceback purpose. This packet marking mechanism is currently a dominant method for IP traceback, and it includes two categories: Probabilistic Packet Marking (PPM) [2] and Deterministic Packet Marking (DPM) [3]. In general, the packet marking based traceback schemes suffer a number of disadvantages, such as scalability, accuracy and depending on attack signatures. The traffic entropy variation based traceback can address some of the problems of packet marking [4].

All the available IP traceback schemes depend on the participation of Internet routers, and the more the better. Moreover, all IP traceback depends on successful DDoS detections. We will study the three categories of IP traceback in the following.

4.2   Probabilistic Packet Marking Based Traceback

The PPM strategy was firstly proposed in [2], and was further improved by researchers, such as in [5].

The basic idea of the PPM scheme is that at participated domains, e.g., ISP networks, special marks are injected into the available packet space of incoming packets with a probability at all routers. At the victim end, we can establish an attack tree based on the received marked packets, and identify the attack sources based on the attack tree T. In order to establish a reliable attack tree, we have to accumulate a large number of marked packets, which causes a challenge on storage and computing power at the victim end. Moreover, the PPM scheme can only trace to the source nodes within its domain, which are usually far away from the attacking bots.

Savage et al. [6] firstly introduced the probability-based packet marking method, node appending, which appends each nodes address to the end of the packet as it travels from the attack source to the victim. Obviously, it is infeasible when the path is long or there is insufficient unused space in the original packet. The authors proposed the node sampling algorithm, which records the router address to the packet with probability, p, on the routers of the attack path. Then, the probability of a packet marked by a router that d hops away from the victim is $p(1-p)^{d-1}$. Based on the number of marked packets, we can reconstruct the attack path. However, it requires large number of packets to improve the accuracy of the attack path reconstruction. Therefore, an edge sampling algorithm was proposed to mark the start router address and end router address of an attack link and the distance between the two ends. The edge sampling algorithm fixed the problems of the node sampling algorithm to some extent.

Based on the PPM mechanism, in [7], the traffic that targeted the victim was measured to construct the attack diagram, and then identified where the attackers were located. They focused on the traffic flows, which ended at the victim, and therefore, there was a tree which was rooted at the victim. For a router on the attack tree, the outgoing flow included two parts: the locally generated flows and the transit flows from the upstream router(s) of the attack tree. If X_1 and X_2 are two flows on the attack tree, and X_1 is the upstream flow of X_2, then $Pr\{X_1 > x\} \geq Pr\{X_2 > x\}$, for any x. The victim will collect all the marked packets from the routers and reconstruct the attack tree based on the traffic rates of different routers. This traceback method heavily depends on the queuing model, and it requires the traffic flows to obey specific patterns, e.g., the Poisson distribution.

In [5], the randomize-and-link approach to implement IP traceback based on the probabilistic packet marking mechanism was proposed. The algorithm targets two aspects: to reconstruct the marks from the marker efficiently and to make the PPM more secure against hackers' pollution. The idea is to have every router X to fragment its unique message M_x (e.g., IP address) into several pieces, $M_0, M_1; \ldots M_l$. At the same time, the router calculates the checksum $C = C(M_x)$, named as *cord*. The router assembles the mark as b_i, and injects b_i randomly into the unused IPv4 packet header (say, N bits, which is 25 bits in the paper: 16 bits of fragmentation ID, 1 bit of the fragmentation index, and 8 bits of service type, all of them are used rarely in a common IPv4 packet). The b_i includes three parts: an index of the pieces ($\ln l$ bits), a large checksum $C = C(M_x)(N - \ln l - |M_i|)$ bits, and a piece of

M_i, $i = 0, 1, \ldots$ ($|M_i|$ bits). The cord is quite large, for example, 14 out of 25 bits, therefore, we can treat the cord as a random number, which is hard for hackers to predict. The victim can reconstruct the message efficiently by checking the cord and the index sequence.

Yaar et al. [8] studied the marking technique to improve the PPM mechanism. They broke the 16-bits marking space into three parts: 1 bit for distance, 2 bits for fragmentation index, and a hash fragmentation of 13 bits. By this modification, the proposed FIT algorithm can traceback the attack paths with high probability after receiving only tens of packets. The FIT algorithm also performed well even in the presence of legacy routers and it is a scalable algorithm for thousands of attack sources.

Snoeren et al. [9] proposed a method by logging packets or digests of packets at routers. The packets are digested using bloom filter at all the routers. Based on these logged information, the victim can traceback the leaves on an attack tree. The methods can even traceback a single packet. However, it also places a significant strain on the storage capability of intermediate routers.

In [10], two hybrid schemes, Distributed Link-List Traceback (DLLT) and the Probabilistic Pipelined Packet Marking (PPPM), which combine the packet marking and packet logging method to traceback the attack sources are proposed. The first one preserves the marking information at intermediate routers in a specific way so that it can be collected using a link-list-based approach. The second algorithm targets propagating the IP addresses of the routers that were involved in marking certain packets by loading them into packets going to the same destination, therefore, preserving these addresses while avoiding the need for long-term storage at the intermediate routers.

At the end of this subsection, we list the disadvantages of PPM based traceback schemes.

1. First of all, the PPM strategy targets on traceback at the victim end, and it only operate in a local range of the Internet where the victim seats. Due to the anarchy nature of the Internet, it is very difficult to organize a large collaboration among different ISPs. Therefore, PPM is carried out generally within a small range, and we cannot traceback to the attack sources located out of the controlled domains.
2. Secondly, as attackers can send spoofed marking information to the victim to mislead the victim. The accuracy of PPM is another problem because the marked messages by the routers who are closer to the leaves (which means far away from the victim) could be overwritten by the downstream routers on the attack tree.
3. Thirdly, most of the PPM algorithms suffer from the storage space problem on storing a large amount of marked packets for reconstructing the attack tree.
4. Fourthly, PPM requires a large number of Internet routers to participate in the traceback process.

4.3 Deterministic Packet Marking Based Traceback

Different from the PPM method, the DPM scheme deploys a deterministic method and tries to mark packets at routers that are the closest to attack sources (ideally, at the router of the LAN where bots stay). This scheme was firstly proposed by Belenky and Ansari [3], and then further developed in [1, 11]. A victim can identify an attack source with a few marked packets from the same source under the DPM scheme. The DPM schemes relax the pressure on storage and computing power at the victim side compared to that of the PPM schemes.

Belenky and Ansari [3] noticed that the PPM mechanism can only solve large flooding attacks, and it is not applicable for attacks consisted of a small number of packets. Therefore, they proposed a deterministic packet marking method for IP traceback. The basic idea was that at the initial router of an information source, the router embedded its IP address into the packet by chopping the router's IP into two segments with 17 bits each (16 bits for half of the IP address and 1 bit worked as index). As a result, the victim can trace which router the packets came from.

In general, there are three possible units of an IPv4 packet: Fragment ID (16 bits), Reserved Flag (1 bit), and Type of Service (TOS in short, 8 bits). The original DPM scheme used 17 bits for marking (Fragment ID and Reserved Flag), and the FDPM scheme used 24 bits (Fragment ID and TOS) as a maximum length and 16 bits (Fragment ID) as the least length. We refer reader to [3, 11] and [1] for the reason why these space can be used for marking.

The basic idea of encoding of the DPM mechanism is as follows. As show in Fig. 4.2, we suppose the available marking space is $l(l = 1, 2, \ldots)$. In the DPM· encoding schemes, l is split into three parts: d (d for ID) bits are employed to denote an unique ID for an ingress router, and a (a for address) bits are used to carry a part of the IP address of the marking router, and s (s for sequence) bits are deployed to indicate the sequence or index of the partial IP address. It is obvious that

$$l = a + d + s. \tag{4.1}$$

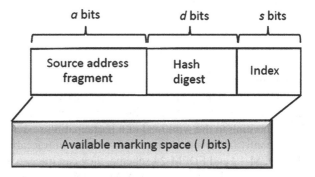

Fig. 4.2 The encoding mechanism of DPM schemes

The constraints of Eq. (4.1) are

$$\begin{cases} a \geq 1 \\ d \geq 1 \\ s \geq 2 \\ 2^s \geq a. \end{cases} \tag{4.2}$$

Usually, we have two important metrics to measure a DPM scheme: Maximum traceable sources N_{max} and storage space N_{store}.

As scalability is an inherent hurdle of the DPM mechanism, therefore, it is always a hot topic of improving N_{max}. Based on Eqs. (4.1) and (4.2), we have

$$N_{max} = 2^d = 2^{l-a-s}. \tag{4.3}$$

The calculation of N_{store} is usually modeled as a coupon collection problem, which is explained as follows.

Suppose there are k $(k \in N)$ unique coupons to be collected. In order to collect all of the them, the total coupons that we have to collect is expressed as follows.

$$k \left(\frac{1}{k} + \frac{1}{k-1} + \ldots + \frac{1}{2} + 1 \right). \tag{4.4}$$

In our case, $k = 2^s$, the storage cost for the DPM schemes is

$$N_{store} = 2^s \left(\frac{1}{2^s} + \frac{1}{2^s - 1} + \ldots + \frac{1}{2} + 1 \right). \tag{4.5}$$

Jin and Yang [12] improved the ID coding of the deterministic packet marking scheme using redundant decomposition of the initial router IP address. For an IP address, they divided them into three redundant segments, 0–13, 9–22, and 18–31 bits, and then five different hash functions were applied on the three segments to create five results. The resulting eight segments are recorded in the outgoing packets randomly. The victim could reassemble the source router IP using the packets it had received.

Xiang et al. [1] noticed the scalability disadvantage of the original DPM scheme, and proposed a flexible deterministic packet marking (FDPM) method to traceback attack sources. They deployed a flexible mark length strategy to match different network environments, and the marking length varied from 16, 19 to 24 bits depending on the underneath network protocols. Moreover, they also designed a flexible flow-based marking scheme to adaptively change the marking rate according to the workload of a participating router in the scheme. The FDPM significantly improved the maximum number of traceable sources. For example, for the FDPM-19 and FDPM-24 scheme, they can trace to 8,192 and 262,144 sources, respectively. While the original DPM scheme can only trace to 2,048 sources.

We also list the limitations of the DPM mechanism at the end of this subsection.

1. First of all, scalability is the greatest challenge for current DPM schemes. As discussed before with only 25 spare bits available in an IPv4 packet, it is impossible to cover every possible source on the Internet.
2. The DPM mechanism poses an extraordinary challenge on storage for packet logging for routers.
3. Similar to the PPM schemes, DPM schemes are vulnerable to packet pollution from hackers.

4.4 Marking on Demand Traceback Scheme

The maximum number of traceable sources (N_{max}) is a major metric for various existing DPM schemes. As described in [5], there are at least two million routers on the Internet, and the current DPM schemes cannot cover all the possible routers. Defenders can only trace 2,048 sources in the original DPM scheme [3]. To date, the best result in this aspect is 262,144 traceable sources from the Flexible DPM scheme [1]. This means we can only traceback around 10 % of the total possible attack sources in terms of routers using the best available DPM scheme.

The scalability problem of the current DPM schemes roots in its static encoding mechanism. All the current DPM schemes are designed under an implicit assumption: all Internet routers are possibly involved in a DDoS attack. Therefore, they have to assign an unique and static ID for each router of the Internet. However, the available space in IPv4 packet head is limited, and cannot serve the needs of encoding every Internet router an unique ID.

In order to address the scalability problem of DPM mechanism, we proposed a Marking on Demand (MOD) scheme to dynamically assign marking IDs to DDoS attack related routers to perform traceback tasks [13].

The method based on two characteristics of DDoS attacks.

1. In terms of space, most of the current DDoS attacks are organized by botnets [14–16], and for an attack session, the number of bots (compromised computers) involved is at the hundreds or a few thousands level [17]. This means that for every attack, there are only a small number of routers are involved, the IDs that the current DPM schemes assign to the routers that are not involved in attacks are wasted and not necessary.
2. In terms of time, a DDoS attack session is usually short and the attack frequency of a botnet is low [18].

Based on these two facts, we only need to assign unique marks for every attack related router for a given attack session at a given time point. In other words, we can take advantage of different space and different time to significantly extend the scalability feature of the DPM mechanism.

As we know, DDoS attacks usually company with a surge of the number of packets addressed to victims. Due to detection sensitivity, we can detect DDoS attacks only when the increase of attack packets is sufficient. This phenomenon is generally easy to catch at the victim end, but hard to detect at the original LANs where bots seats.

In the proposed traceback framework, we set up a global mark distribution server (MOD server). At every local router or gateway of participant Internet domains, we install a DDoS attack detector to monitor network flows. When there appears suspicious network flows, the detector requests unique IDs from the MOD server, and embeds the assigned unique IDs to mark the packets of suspicious flows. At the same time, the MOD server deposits the IP address of the request router and the assigned marks into its MOD database. Once a victim confirms a DDoS attack, it can extract the unique IDs from the attack packets and search the MOD database to identify the IP addresses of the attack sources.

4.4.1 The Framework of Marking on Demand Scheme

First of all, we make the following definition.

Definition 4.4.1. Network Flow. We define the network packets that share the same destination address and the same source address as a Network Flow or Flow.

Based on this definition, if there are n bots hosted by n different computers in a local area network, and they target on the same victim (the same destination IP address), then there are n attack flows in the system. On the other hand, in the case that one compromised computer hosts multiple different bots, and they pump traffic to m different victims, then we have m flows in the system.

The system diagram of the Marking on Demand framework is shown in Fig. 4.3. In this new framework, we have one global MOD server, which assigns unique marks responding to requests. Moreover, the MOD server also possesses a web based database, which stores the mark information for possible retrieval.

In detail, all the collaborating gateways (ideally all the routers of the Internet) install a DDoS attack detector, which monitors the outgoing network flows. The proposed traceback system works as follows.

1. When there is a suspicious surge of volume of network flows, the monitor submits a request to the MOD server for a unique mark (step 1 in the diagram).
2. The MOD server identifies a unique mark to serve the request, and deposits the related information (the mark, request source IP address, time stamp) into the database (step 2 in the diagram).
3. The gateway will use the assigned mark to pad the suspicious outgoing traffic at the available marking fields.

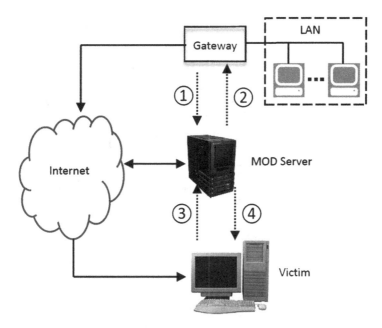

Fig. 4.3 The framework of the marking on demand scheme

4. Once a victim confirms that it is under a DDoS attack, it extracts the marks from the attack packets, and submit a query about the source IP of the related marks (step 3 in the diagram).
5. The MOD server check its database about the marks, and responds the request with the related IP addresses. In this way, the victim knows the attack sources (step 4 in the diagram).

The comparison of the MOD method and the traditional DPM schemes are as follows. As show in Fig. 4.4, in the DPM and the FDPM schemes, the available marking space are split into three parts: d' (d for ID) bits are employed to denote a unique ID for a ingress router, and a' (a for address) bits are used to carry a part of the IP address, and s' (s for sequence) bits are deployed to indicate the sequence of partial IP address.

4.4.2   System Analysis of the MOD Scheme

For the proposed MOD attack source traceback scheme, it is important to understand the attack frequency and attack durations under the whole Internet level.

The available marking length in an IPv4 header is quite important for the performance of every DPM based scheme. Theoretically, in our MOD scheme, we can use 25 bits as the maximum and 16 bits as the least. For the sake of comparison,

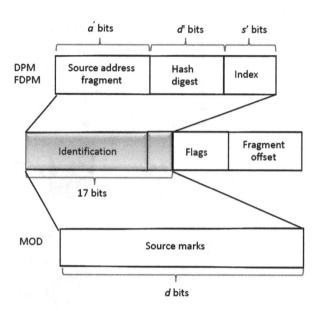

Fig. 4.4 The comparison between the proposed marking on demand scheme with the typical DPM schemes

we take the marking length as 24 bits as the maximum and 16 bits as the minimum for MOD scheme in our analysis and comparison.

For a given time point t, let random variable $A(t)$ be the number of ongoing DDoS attacks, $D(t)$ be the duration for a given attack, and $B(t)$ be the number of bots involving in an attack. For example, let $A_i(t)$ represent the ith attack of $A(t)$, then its duration is denoted as $D_i(t)$ and the its number of bots is $B_i(t)$. Let $N(t)$ be the total number of attack sources on the Internet for any given time point t. Then we have

$$N(t) = \sum_{i=1}^{A(t)} B_i(t) \tag{4.6}$$

Let $E[A(t)]$, $E[B(t)]$, and $E[D(t)]$ be the expectation of random variable $A(t)$, $B(t)$, and $D(t)$ respectively. Based on the Wald Theorem, we have

$$E[N(t)] = E[A(t)] \cdot E[B(t)] \tag{4.7}$$

As the marking space l is limited, therefore, we will run out of unique IDs for marking as DDoS attacks are continuously organized by hackers. Let T_I (I stands for time interval) be the time interval that we can assign unique IDs, then the number of unique marks that we have for traceback needs during this time interval is

$$E[N(t)] \cdot \frac{T_I}{E[D(t)]}. \tag{4.8}$$

Table 4.1 Quantity comparison among the MOD scheme with the DPM and the FDPM schemes

Scheme	Maximum traceable source	Marked packet required	Storage required
DPM-17	2^{11}	32	129.87
FDPM-16	2^{10}	32	129.87
FDPM-24	2^{18}	32	129.87
MOD-16	2^{16}	1	1
MOD-17	2^{17}	1	1
MOD-24	2^{24}	1	1

Table 4.2 Key statistics on DDoS attack characteristics

Feature	Attack frequency [18]	Attack duration [18]	Attack rate [18]	Sources per attack session [17]
Value	6,272/h	5 min	500 pkts/s	Around 1,000

The quantity comparison among the MOD, the DPM, and the FDPM schemes is summarized in Table 4.1.

From Table 4.1, we can see that in terms of maximum number of traceable sources, the MOD scheme is 64 (2^6) times of that of the DPM or the FDPM schemes with the same available marking space. At the same time, we note that the storage cost for achieving the N_{max} for the DPM scheme and the FDPM scheme are around 132 times of that of the MOD scheme. More importantly, the MOD scheme can achieve single packet traceback.

We summarize the key statistics of DDoS attacks in a global scenario from highly referred literature [17, 18], and present them in Table 4.2.

For a given time point t, we can calculate the average number of active bots using the following equation.

$$E[N(t)] = \frac{E[A(t)] \cdot E[B(t)]}{E[D(t)]} \tag{4.9}$$

Combining Eq. (4.9) and the parameters in Table 4.2, we can estimate the number of concurrent active bots in attacking around 523,000. We note that this number is the active bots from different botnets and from different network domains.

Recall that our target is to identify the routers, which are the closest to bots. In other words, we are interested to know how many domains, $N_d(t)$, are involved in an attack session at time t given $N(t)$. With $N_d(t)$ in hands, we can arrange our encoding for traceback. In order to calculate $N_d(t)$ from $N(t)$, we need one more information on distribution of bots in terms of domain. To date, researchers are not clear about the distribution except that it is a non-uniform distribution [19]. At the same time, people found that the size distribution usually follows the power law, such as population in cities in a country or personal income in a nation [20, 21].

Therefore, it is acceptable that we assume the size distribution of botnets follows the power law for the analysis. Further, we use the Zipf distribution as an instance of the power law, which is defined as follows.

$$Pr\{x = i\} = \frac{C}{i^\alpha},\qquad(4.10)$$

where α is a positive parameter, $Pr\{x = i\}$ represents the probability of the ith $(i = 1, 2, \ldots)$ largest botnet in terms of size, and $\sum_i Pr\{x = i\} = 1$.

Suppose at a given time point t, the concurrent $N(t)$ bots come from k LANs, namely we need to traceback to k routers in this case. If we sort the k LANs in terms of size in a decent style. Let the kth LAN only hosts one bot. Then the parameter k is decided by the following conditions.

$$\begin{cases} C = \frac{1}{\sum_{i=1}^{k} i^\alpha}, \\[2mm] 1 = \frac{C}{k^\alpha} \cdot N(t). \end{cases}\qquad(4.11)$$

In a simple form, k is decided by

$$N(t) = k^\alpha \cdot \sum_{i=1}^{k} i^\alpha\qquad(4.12)$$

Taking $N(t)$ as 523,000, we shown the relationship between α and k (number of routers involved in a global level of traceback) in Fig. 4.5. We can see from this experiments that the routers involved in DDoS attacks within the whole Internet is around a couple of hundreds level for a given time point. This finding is important for us to relax our pressure of marking resource. At the same time, this finding supports the wide application of the MOD scheme for IP traceback.

Based on Eq. (4.8), we know T_I depends on attack duration ($D(t)$), the number of different LANs involved in an attack (k) and the length of the available marking space (l).

$$T_I = \frac{2^l}{k} \cdot D(t).\qquad(4.13)$$

We are interested to know the time interval (T_I) of running out of marking space in various conditions. It is easy to see from Eq. (4.13) that $E[T_I]$ is proportional to the average attack duration $E[D(t)]$. A shorter $E[D(t)]$ exhausts the marking space faster. Given a reasonable $D(t)$, we want to estimate T_I on the variation of the number of LANs involved in attacks. Figure 4.6 presents a rough idea on T_I.

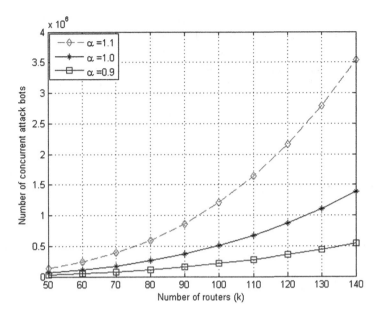

Fig. 4.5 The relationship between parameter α and the number of routers to be traced

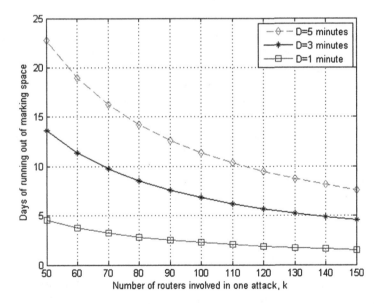

Fig. 4.6 The relationship among T_l and the number of concurrent attack LANs (k) and the average attack duration (D) in the case of marking space $l = 16$

From Fig. 4.6, we can see that the 16 bits marking space can last more than 1.5 days in a relatively strict condition: $k = 150$ and $E[D] = 1$ min. This means that we need to reuse the same ID around every 1.5 days. This may cause problems in terms of accuracy. We can assign unique marks for more than 10 days in a reasonable condition: $k = 110$ and $E[D] = 5$ min. Usually, a DDoS attack does not last that long (10 days). We also note that for the $l = 24$ case, the T_l is around 256 (2^8) times longer than that of $l = 16$ case. In this case, the accuracy issue is dramatically improved.

4.5 Network Traffic Based IP Traceback

In our previous work [4], we proposed a novel mechanism for IP traceback using information theoretical parameters, and there is no packet marking in the proposed strategy. Using this new strategy, we can avoid the inherited shortcomings of the packet marking mechanisms.

The method is flow based and works at the network layer. The definition of flow is a bit different from the previous ones. In this context, the flow is defined as follows.

Definition 4.5.1. Flow. For a given router, the packets, which come from the same upstream router and share the same destination IP address, are categorized as one flow.

In the traceback strategy, we use flow entropy variation or entropy variation interchangeably. Once a DDoS attack has been identified, the victim initiates the following pushback process to identify the locations of zombies: the victim first identifies which of its upstream routers are in the attack tree based on the flow entropy variations it has accumulated, and then submits requests to the related immediate upstream routers. The upstream routers identify where the attack flows came from based on their local entropy variations that they have monitored. Once the immediate upstream routers have identified the attack flows, they will forward the requests to their immediate upstream routers, respectively, to identify the attacker sources further. This procedure is repeated in a parallel and distributed fashion until it reaches the attack source(s) or the discrimination limit between attack flows and legitimate flows is satisfied.

The analysis, experiments, and simulations demonstrate that the entropy variation based traceback mechanism is effective and efficient compared with the existing methods [7, 18]. In particular, it possesses the following advantages.

1. The strategy is fundamentally different from the existing PPM or DPM traceback mechanisms, and it outperforms the available PPM and DPM methods. Because of this essential change, the strategy overcomes the inherited drawbacks of packet marking methods, such as limited scalability, huge demands on storage space, and vulnerability to packet pollution.

2. The implementation of the method brings no modifications on current routing software. Both PPM and DPM require update on the existing routing software, which is extremely hard to achieve on the Internet. On the other hand, our method can work independently as an additional module on routers for monitoring and recording flow information, and communicating with its upstream and downstream routers when the pushback procedure is carried out.
3. The method will be effective for future packet flooding DDoS attacks because it is independent of traffic patterns. Some previous works [7] depend heavily on traffic patterns to conduct their traceback. For example, they expected that traffic patterns obey Poisson distribution or Normal distribution. However, traffic patterns have no impact on the scheme; therefore, we can deal with any complicated attack patterns, even legitimate traffic pattern mimicking attacks.
4. The method can archive real-time traceback to attackers. Once the short-term flow information is in place at routers, and the victim notices that it is under attack, it will start the traceback procedure. The workload of traceback is distributed, and the overall traceback time mainly depends on the network delays between the victim and the attackers.

4.5.1   System Model for IP Traceback on Entropy Variations

In order to clearly describe our traceback mechanism, we use Fig. 4.7 as a sample network with DDoS attacks to demonstrate our traceback strategy. In a DDoS attack scenario, as shown in Fig. 4.7, the flows with destination as the victim include legitimate flows, such as f_3, and a combination of attack flows and legitimate flows, such as f_1 and f_2. Compared with non-attack cases, the volumes of some flows increase significantly in a very short period of time in DDoS attack cases. Observers at routers R_1, R_4, R_5, and V will notice the dramatic changes. However, the routers who are not on the attack paths, such as R_2 and R_3, will not be able to sense the variations. Therefore, once the victim realizes an ongoing attack, it can pushback to the LANs, which caused the changes based on the information of flow entropy variations, and therefore, we can identify the locations of attackers.

The traceback can be done in a parallel and distributed fashion in the scheme. In Fig. 4.7, based on its knowledge of entropy variations, the victim knows that attackers are somewhere behind router R_1, and no attackers are behind router R_2. Then the traceback request is delivered to router R_1. Similar to the victim, router R_1 knows that there are two groups of attackers, one group is behind the link to LAN_0 and another group is behind the link to LAN_1. Then the traceback requests are further delivered to the edge routers of LAN_0 and LAN_1, respectively. Based on entropy variation information of router R_3, the edge router of LAN_0 can infer that the attackers are located in the local area network, LAN_0. Similarly, the edge router of LAN_1 finds that there are attackers in LAN_1; furthermore, there are attackers behind

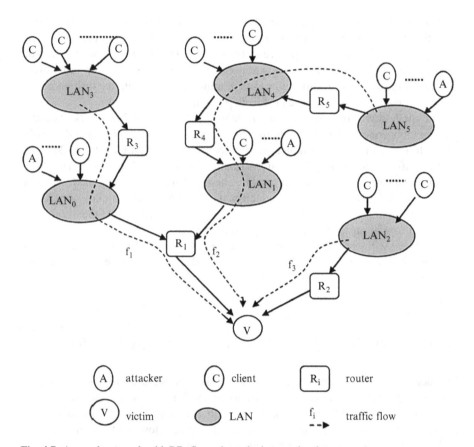

Fig. 4.7 A sample network with DDoS attacks at the internet level

router R_4. The traceback request is then further passed to the upstream routers, until we locate the attackers in LAN_5.

Entropy is an information theoretic concept, which is a measure of randomness. We employ entropy variation to measure changes of randomness of flows at a router for a given time interval. We note that entropy variation is only one of the possible metrics. Chen and Hwang used a statistical feature, change point of flows, to identify the abnormality of DDoS attacks [22]. However, attackers could cheat the feature by increasing attack strength slowly. We can also employ other statistic metrics to measure the randomness, such as standard variation or high-order moments of flows. We choose entropy variation rather than others because of the low computing workload for entropy variations.

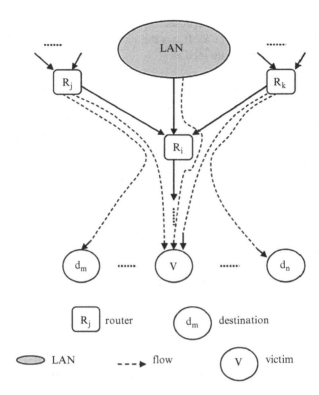

Fig. 4.8 Traffic flows at a router on an attack path

4.5.2 System Analysis on the Model

Let us have a close investigation on the flows of a router, as shown in Fig. 4.8 Generally, a router knows its local topology, e.g., its upstream routers, the local area network attached to the router, and the downstream routers.

We name the router that we are investigating as a *local router*. We denote a flow on a local router by $< u_i, d_j, t >, i, j \in I, t \in R$, where u_i is an upstream router of a local router R_i, d_j is the destination address of a group of packets that are passing through the local router R_i, and t is the current time stamp. For example, the local router R_i in Fig. 4.8 has two different incoming flows – the ones from the upstream routers R_j and R_k, respectively. We name this kind of flows as *transit* flows. Another type of incoming flows of the local router R_i is generated at the local area network, we call these *local flows*, and use L to represent the local flows. We name all the incoming flows as *input flows*, and all the flows leaving router R_i are named as *output flows*. We denote $u_i (i \in I)$ as the immediate upstream routers of the local router R_i, and set U as the set of incoming flows of router R_i. Therefore, $U = \{u_i, i \in I\} + \{L\}$.

We use a set $D = \{d_i, i \in I\}$ to represent the destinations of the packets that are passing through the local router R_i. If v is the victim router, then $v \in D$. Therefore, a flow at a local router can be defined as

$$f_{ij}(u_i, d_j) = \{<u_i, d_j, t> | u_i \in U, d_j \in D, i, j \in I\}. \tag{4.14}$$

We denote $|f_{ij}(u_i, d_j, t)|$ as the count number of packets of the flow f_{ij} at time t. For a given time interval ΔT, we define the variation of the number of packets for a given flow as follows.

$$N_{ij}(u_i, d_j, t + \Delta T) = |f_{ij}(u_i, d_j, t + \Delta T)| - |f_{ij}(u_i, d_j, t)|. \tag{4.15}$$

If we set $|f_{ij}(u_i, d_j, t)| = 0$, then $N_{ij}(u_i, d_j, t + \Delta T)$ is the number of packets of flow f_{ij}, which went through the local router during the time interval ΔT. In order to make the presentation tidy, we use $N_{ij}(u_i, d_j)$ to replace $N_{ij}(u_i, d_j, t + \Delta T)$ in the rest of this section.

Based on the large number theorem, we have the probability of each flow at a local router as

$$p_{ij}(u_i, d_j) = \frac{N_{ij}(u_i, d_j)}{\sum_{i=1}^{\infty} \sum_{j=1}^{\infty} N_{ij}(u_i, d_j)}, \tag{4.16}$$

where $p_{ij}(u_i, d_j)$ gives the probability of the flow f_{ij} over all the flows on the local router, and $\sum_{i=1}^{\infty} \sum_{j=1}^{\infty} p_{ij} = 1$.

Let F be a random variable of the number of flows during the time interval ΔT on a local router, therefore, we define the entropy of flows for the local router as follows.

$$H(F) = -\sum_{ij} p_{ij}(u_i, d_j) \log p_{ij}(u_i, d_j). \tag{4.17}$$

In order to differentiate from the original definition of entropy, we call $H(F)$ *flow entropy*, which measures the variations of randomness of flows on a given local router.

For a local router, suppose that the number of flows is N, and the probability distribution is $\{p_1, p_2, \ldots, p_N\}$. We can simplify the expression of entropy of (4.17) as follows.

$$H(F) = H(p_1, p_2, \ldots, p_N) = -\sum_{i=1}^{N} p_i \log p_i. \tag{4.18}$$

Based on the characteristics of the entropy function, we obtain the upper bound and lower bound of $H(F)$ as follows.

$$0 \leq H(F) \leq \log N. \tag{4.19}$$

We reach the lower bound when $p_i = 1, 1 \leq i \leq N, p_k = 0, k = 1, 2, \ldots, N$, and $k \neq i$. We have the upper bound when $p_1 = p_2 = \ldots = p_N$.

Based on our definition of the random variable of flows, we have the following special cases to reach the lower bound and the upper bound, respectively. When there is only one flow alive during the sampling time interval, and there are no packets going through the local router for the other flows, $H(F) = 0$. When the number of packets for each flow is the same among all the flows at a local router, then we have $H(F) = \log N$.

We divide our time line into two segments for the following investigation: before DDoS attack and under DDoS attack. The local router's flow entropy is, therefore, denoted by $H^-(F)$ and $H^+(F)$, respectively. Let δ be a reasonable threshold, and C be the mean of $H^-(F)$, and the standard variation of $H^-(F)$ be δ. We know that $H^-(F)$ is quite stable for a long time period. We justify our threshold δ to make the following equation holds with high probability,

$$|H^-(F) - C| \leq \delta. \tag{4.20}$$

In order to make the mean C and standard variation δ adaptive to the network traffic variations, let

$$\begin{cases} C[t] = \sum_{i=1}^n \alpha_i C[t-i], \ \sum_{i=1}^n \alpha_i = 1, \\ \delta[t] = \sum_{i=1}^n \beta_i \delta[t-i], \ \sum_{i=1}^n \beta_i = 1, \end{cases} \tag{4.21}$$

where $C[t]$ represents the current mean, $C[t-i]$ is the mean of the ith sample instance in the near past, and $\alpha_i (i = 1, 2, \ldots, n)$ are the weights for the n past samples, respectively. In order to reflect the nearest changes, let $\alpha_i > \alpha_j$ for $i < j, i, j \in I$. The values of α_i are fixed and could be decided by the experiments of non-attack cases. The same for $\delta[t]$, $\delta[t-i]$, and β_i, respectively. The evolutions will be suspended when a DDoS attack is ongoing.

If an attack flow is going through a local router, then the following equation holds with high probability,

$$|H^-(F) - C| > \delta. \tag{4.22}$$

Moreover, we know that the reason behind this is that the packet numbers of flows $< u_i, v > (u_i \in U)$ increase significantly. In order to find the immediate sources of the attack flows from the upstream routers, we sort the flows $< u_i, v > (u_i \in U)$ in terms of number of packets of a given attack flow, $N_{iv}(u_i, v)$. We calculate the flow entropy reiteratively by taking the suspicious flows out starting with the flow that has the greatest packet number, until the difference between the flow entropy of the remaining flows and the mean is less than or equal to the threshold, δ. In other words, the process stops when the following equation holds,

$$|H^+(F \setminus max(\{< u_i, v >\})) - C| \leq \delta, \tag{4.23}$$

where $F \setminus max(\{< u_i, v >\})$ means taking the maximum element of set $\{< u_i, v >\}$ from set F. Then the subset $\{u_i\} \subseteq U$, which includes the upstream routers that we have taken out before Eq. (4.23) holds, is the set of suspicious immediate sources of the DDoS attack. Then the traceback requests are further forwarded to the elements of set $\{u_i\}$, respectively. The traceback processing terminates under the following conditions.

$$\begin{cases} L = max(\{< u_i, v >\}), \\ |H^+(F \setminus L - C)| \le \delta. \end{cases} \qquad (4.24)$$

Then L, the flows of the local area network, is the attack source of that branch on the attack tree.

References

1. Y. Xiang, W. Zhou, and M. Guo, "Flexible deterministic packet marking: An ip traceback system to find the real source of attacks," *IEEE Transactions on Parallel and Distributed Systems*, vol. 20, no. 4, pp. 567–580, 2009.
2. S. Savage, D. Wetherall, A. R. Karlin, and T. E. Anderson, "Practical network support for ip traceback," in *Proceedings of the SIGCOMM*, 2000, pp. 295–306.
3. A. Belenky and N. Ansari, "Ip traceback with deterministic packet marking," *IEEE Communications Letters*, vol. 7, no. 4, pp. 162–164, 2003.
4. S. Yu, W. Zhou, R. Doss, and W. Jia, "Traceback of ddos attacks using entropy variations," *IEEE Transactions on Parallel and Distributed Systems*, vol. 22, no. 3, pp. 412–425, 2011.
5. M. T. Goodrich, "Probabilistic packet marking for large-scale ip traceback," *IEEE/ACM Transactions on Networking*, vol. 16, no. 1, pp. 15–24, 2008.
6. S. Savage, D. Wetherall, A. R. Karlin, and T. E. Anderson, "Network support for ip traceback," *IEEE/ACM Transactions on Networking*, vol. 9, no. 3, pp. 226–237, 2001.
7. T. K. T. Law, J. C. S. Lui, and D. K. Y. Yau, "You can run, but you can't hide: An effective statistical methodology to trace back ddos attackers," *IEEE Transactions on Parallel and Distributed Systems*, vol. 16, no. 9, pp. 799–813, 2005.
8. A. Yaar, A. Perrig, and D. X. Song, "Fit: fast internet traceback," in *Proceedings of the INFOCOM*, 2005, pp. 1395–1406.
9. A. C. Snoeren, C. Partridge, L. A. Sanchez, C. E. Jones, F. Tchakountio, B. Schwartz, S. T. Kent, and W. T. Strayer, "Single-packet ip traceback," *IEEE/ACM Transactions on Networking*, vol. 10, no. 6, pp. 721–734, 2002.
10. B. Al-Duwairi and G. Manimaran, "Novel hybrid schemes employing packet marking and logging for ip traceback," *IEEE Transactions on Parallel and Distributed Systems*, vol. 17, no. 5, pp. 403–418, 2006.
11. A. Belenky and N. Ansari, "On deterministic packet marking," *Computer Networks*, vol. 51, no. 10, pp. 2677–2700, 2007.
12. G. Jin and J. Yang, "Deterministic packet marking based on redundant decomposition for ip traceback," *IEEE Communications Letters*, vol. 10, no. 3, pp. 204–206, 2006.
13. S. Yu, W. Zhou, S. Guo, and M. Guo, "A dynamical deterministic packet marking scheme for ddos traceback," in *Proceedings of the IEEE Globecom*, 2013.
14. V. L. L. Thing, M. Sloman, and N. Dulay, "A survey of bots used for distributed denial of service attacks," in *Proceedings of the SEC*, 2007, pp. 229–240.

15. S. Yu, S. Guo, and I. Stojmenovic, "Can we beat legitimate cyber behavior mimicking attacks from botnets?" in *Proceedings of the INFOCOM*, 2012.
16. S. Yu, W. Zhou, W. Jia, S. Guo, Y. Xiang, and F. Tang, "Discriminating ddos attacks from flash crowds using flow correlation coefficient," *IEEE Transactions on Parallel Distributed Systems*, vol. 23, no. 6, pp. 794–805, 2012.
17. M. A. Rajab, J. Zarfoss, F. Monrose, and A. Terzis, "My botnet is bigger than yours (maybe, better than yours): why size estimates remain challenging," in *Proceedings of the first conference on Hot Topics in Understanding Botnets*, 2007.
18. D. Moore, C. Shannon, D. J. Brown, G. M. Voelker, and S. Savage, "Inferring internet denial-of-service activity," *ACM Transactions on Computer Systems*, vol. 24, no. 2, pp. 115–139, 2006.
19. Z. Chen and C. Ji, "An information-theoretic view of network-aware malware attacks," *IEEE Transactions on Information Forensics and Security*, vol. 4, no. 3, pp. 530–541, 2009.
20. R. L. Axtell, "Zipf distribution of u.s. firm sizes," *Science*, vol. 293, 2001.
21. M. Mitzenmacher, "A brief history of generative models for power law and lognornal distributions," *Internet Mathematics*, vol. 1, 2004.
22. Y. Chen and K. Hwang, "Collaborative detection and filtering of shrew ddos attacks using spectral analysis," *Journal of Parallel and Distributed Computing*, vol. 66, no. 9, pp. 1137–1151, Sep. 2006.

Chapter 5
DDoS Attack and Defence in Cloud

Abstract In this chapter, we explore DDoS attack and defence in the incoming dominant cloud computing platform. We firstly answer the question whether we can beat DDoS attacks in cloud with its current attack capability or not, and the cost for countering the attacks. We also discuss a possible architecture of cloud firewall against DDoS attacks.

5.1 Introduction

Today, cloud computing has become one of the fastest growing sectors in the IT industry all over the world. Cloud computing features a cost-efficient, "pay-as-you-go" business model and flexible architectures, such as SaaS, PaaS and SaaS [1]. A cloud platform can dynamically clone virtual machines in a very quick fashion, e.g. duplicating a gigabyte level server within 1 min [2]. Despite the promising business model and hype surrounding cloud computing, security is the major concern for businesses shifting their applications to clouds [3, 4].

After so many years, defenders have realized that it is essentially a resource competition problem in DDoS attack and defence, and the winner is the one who possesses more resources than his opponent. For a non-cloud environment, the current DDoS mitigation techniques depend on either sufficiency of resource or collaboration among different organizations. On top of a large number of attack packets, a DDoS attack may be carried out in various forms. As a result, our detection has to go through many different possible detection methods, such as IP spoofing [5], hop-count [6], packet score [7], and flash crowd mimicking [8, 9]. Therefore, DDoS detection is expensive in terms of computing power.

Yau et al. [10] viewed DDoS attacks as a resource management issue in their DDoS defence proposal. They proposed the installation of a router throttle at selected upstream routers of a possible victim. The participant routers regulate the traffic flows to the protected server in a proactive way using a level-k max-min fairness strategy. Their target was to constrain the number of attack packets far

S. Yu, *Distributed Denial of Service Attack and Defense*, SpringerBriefs in Computer   77
Science, DOI 10.1007/978-1-4614-9491-1__5, © The Author(s) 2014

away from the protected server. If we have sufficient resources, such as bandwidth and computing power, we can then perform a deep packet inspection, and filter out attack packets. However, this is not usually possible for a non-cloud platform. Chen et al. [11] proposed a DDoS attack mitigation scheme, attack diagnosis (AD), using a divide-and-conquer strategy to address the problem. They used the push back strategy to enable an AD to work as close as possible to an individual attack source. As a result, attack sources were isolated, and then throttled. Another method is to establish an ally among multiple network domains to protect a potential victim. In [12], distributed change-point detection architecture was proposed using a change aggregation tree (CAT). Each CAT works at one network domain, and all CATs report their traffic fluctuation to a server, with the server overlooking all the reports to make a final decision on DDoS attacks. The authors of [13] proposed FireCol, a distributed intrusion prevention system at the ISP level to mitigate DDoS attacks from large botnets. The cooperative ISPs establish virtual protection rings around potential victims to defend and collaborate through the exchange of selected traffic information. However, it is difficult to obtain either sufficient resources or collaboration among multiple network domains in a non-cloud environment at the Internet level.

For us, we are interested to answer the following question: How can we defeat DDoS attacks in the cloud environment. A cloud infrastructure provider pools a large amount of resources and makes them easy access in order to handle a rapid increase in service demands [1]. Therefore, it is almost impossible for a DDoS attack to shut down a cloud. However, individual cloud customers (referred to as parties hosting their services in a cloud) cannot escape from DDoS attacks nowadays as they usually do not have the advantage.

A variation of a DDoS attack in cloud computing is the Economic Denial of Sustainability (EDoS) attack [14] or the Fraudulent Resource Consumption (FRC) attack [15]. If the billing mechanism for cloud customers is "pay-as-you-use", botnet owners can create a large number of fake users to intensively consume the service of the targeted cloud customer. For example, the existing flash crowd mimicking attacks [8, 16] on an e-business web site is an excellent example. As a result, the bill for the targeted cloud customer will increase dramatically until the victim suspends her service or is bankrupted. On the other hand, if a cloud customer fixes her cost for renting the resources of her hosted services, then an effective DDoS attack will disturb, or even shut her services down.

There has been some work on mitigating DDoS attacks in a cloud computing environment. Lua and Yow [17] proposed the establishment of a large swarm network to mitigate DDoS attacks on a cloud, with an intelligent fast-flux technique used to transparently maintain connectivity between nodes in a swarm network, cloud clients and servers. Their software simulation indicated they can maintain a high percentage of benign request delivery rates while successfully blocking attack packets. Chen et al. [18] proposed on-demand security architecture to offer different services for different needs in cloud environments. This includes three factors: risk of network access, service type and security level. Based on the mechanism of cloud computing, this is a good idea as it meets the different requirements of users.

Table 5.1 Amazon EC2 pricing for standard on-demand instances

Instance Type	Linux (per hour)	Windows (per hour)
Small (default)	$0.060	$0.115
Medium	$0.120	$0.230
Large	$0.240	$0.460
Extra large	$0.480	$0.920

In order to deal with EDoS attacks, Sqalli et al. [14] proposed a white and black list based filtering scheme to block malicious service requests. Amazon developed cloudWatch [19], a tool to monitor the company's cloud resources and mitigate EDoS attacks on their cloud customers.

Different from other computing platforms, a cloud data centre usually possesses a significant amount of computing power and bandwidth. For example, Amazon EC2 has almost 500,000 servers, and small instances on a server usually share 1 G bits bandwidth. In terms of financial cost, it is far cheaper to establish a web based application within a cloud environment compared with the traditional way. In a cloud, an instance is a basic unit for renting, and it is equivalent to a PC or a server. We list the latest pricing of Amazon EC2 Pricing for Standard On-Demand Instances [20] in Table 5.1.

Moreover, cloud platforms possess the unique feature of cloning virtual machines on the fly. Of course, there is a cost for performing this function. In general, there are two categories for cloning virtual machines in a cloud: the network-driven approach and the non-network efforts. For the first group, researchers usually take a BitTorrent-like strategy to treat an image of a virtual machine as one file, and distribute the entire file as demanded [21]. In the second category, researchers try to take advantage of non-network techniques, such as reducing the size of a virtual machine image, prediction and partial page launch to speed up the initialization of virtual machine instances [22]. Peng et al. [2] observed six production cloud data centers for a long period of time, and proposed a chunk-level, network topology-aware virtual machine image distribution network. The proposed method can reduce the cloning time with the 1 min level.

As we have discussed in previous chapters, due to the anti-virus and anti-malware effort and software, the number of active bots a botmaster can manipulate is constrained to the hundreds or few thousands level, even though the number of bot footprints may be much larger. Therefore, the attacking resource for botnet owners is limited. As a result, it is possible for defenders to win the battle in cloud environment taking advantage of the unique features of cloud platforms.

5.2   Defeat DDoS Attacks in Cloud

In our previous work [23], we proposed a practical dynamic resource allocation mechanism to confront DDoS attacks that target individual cloud customers. In general, there is one or several access points between a cloud data center and the Internet. Similar to firewalls, we place our Intrusion Prevention System (IPS) at these locations to monitor incoming packets. When a cloud hosted server is under a DDoS attack, the proposed mechanism will automatically and dynamically allocate extra resources from the available cloud resource pool, and new virtual machines will be cloned based on the image file of the original IPS using the existing clone technology [21, 22]. All IPSs will work together to filter attack packets out, and guarantee the quality of service (QoS) for benign users at the same time. When the volume of DDoS attack packets decreases, our mitigation system will automatically reduce the number of its IPSs, and release the extra resources back to the available cloud resource pool.

As aforementioned, the essential issue to defeat a DDoS attack is to allocate sufficient resources to mitigate attacks no mater how efficient our detection and filtering algorithms are. In order to estimate our resource demands and QoS for benign users in a DDoS battle, we employ queueing theory to undertake performance evaluation due to its extensive deployment in could performance analysis, such as in [24].

First of all, we examine the features of a cloud hosted virtual server in a non-attack scenario. As shown in Fig. 5.1a, similar to an independent Internet based service, a cloud hosted service includes a server, an intrusion prevention system (IPS in the diagram), and a buffer for incoming packets (queue Q in the diagram). The IPS is used to protect the specific server of the hosted service. All packets of benign users go through the queue, pass the IPS and are served by the server. In general, the number of benign users is stable, and we suppose the virtual IPS and virtual server have been allocated sufficient resources, and therefore the quality of service (QoS) is satisfactory to users.

When a DDoS attack occurs against the hosted virtual server, a large number of attack packets are generated by botnets, and pumped to queue Q. In order to identify these attack packets and guarantee the QoS of benign users, we have to invest more resources to clone multiple IPSs to carry out the task. We proposed to clone multiple parallel IPSs to achieve the goal as shown in Fig. 5.1b.

The number of IPSs we need to achieve our goal depends on the volume of the attack packets. As discussed previously, the attack capability of a botnet is usually limited, and the required amount of resources to beat the attack is usually not very large. In general, it is reasonable to expect a cloud can manage its reserved or idle resources to meet demand.

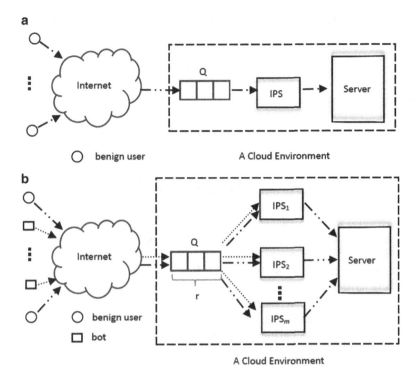

Fig. 5.1 (**a**) A cloud hosted server in a non-attack scenario. (**b**) A cloud hosted server under DDoS attack with the mitigation strategy in place

5.2.1   System Model in General

In general, we treat our studied system as a black box, and observe its input and output with respect of time t. We denote the input as $a(t)$, the output as $b(t)$, and the system function of the black box as $h(t)$. We then have a relationship among these three functions as follows.

$$b(t) = a(t) * h(t), \qquad (5.1)$$

where $*$ is the convolution operation.

In order to obtain solutions for the output, and for most of the cases, we map $a(t)$ and $h(t)$ into another domain using different transform techniques, such as Laplace-transform, Z-transform, and so on. We use the Laplace transform here. The Laplace transform of $a(t)$ is defined as follows.

$$A(s) \triangleq \int a(t)e^{-st}\,dt \qquad (5.2)$$

Similarly, we can obtain $H(s)$ from $h(t)$. Let $B(s)$ be the Laplace transform of $b(t)$, and we obtain $B(s)$ through the following equation.

$$B(s) = A(s) \cdot H(s) \tag{5.3}$$

Once $B(s)$ is in place, we can calculate $b(t)$ using the inverse Laplace transform,

$$b(t) = \frac{1}{2\pi i} \int B(s) e^{st} \, ds \tag{5.4}$$

In our case, $a(t)$ represents the arrival distribution, $h(t)$ is the system service distribution. In the queueing theory, our studied system can be modeled as $G/G/m$, namely, general arrival distribution and general service rate distribution. However, for this general model, the analysis will be very complex, and we may not have computationally attractable methods to calculate the numerical results of these models [25]. For example, we cannot obtain $A(s)$, $H(s)$ from $a(t)$, $h(t)$ most of the time, and we cannot obtain $b(t)$ even if $B(s)$ is in place sometimes. As a result, researchers have to approximate the complex $G/G/m$ model to solvable models in order to proceed with analysis and prediction. To date, only the $M/M/m$ model (exponential arrival rate and service rate) can offer a closed form result as these distributions possess wonderful properties, such as additive and memoryless [26]. We will also follow this mainstream method for our analysis on the proposed mitigation strategy.

5.2.2 Approximation of the Model

As widely applied in cloud performance analysis [24], we make a few reasonable assumptions and approximations in order to make our modelling and analysis feasible and practical. There are:

- Whether or not there is a DDoS attack, we suppose the number of benign users is stable, and we suppose the cloud is big enough and has sufficient reserved or idle resources to overcome a DDoS attack on a cloud customer.
- We suppose the arrival rate to the system follows the Poisson distribution when a DDoS attack is ongoing. We know the arrivals of a server in a non-attack case obey the Poisson distribution. When a DDoS attack is ongoing, there are many more packets to the system, and a general conclusion from queueing theory is that a large number of arrival rate can be approximated as a Poisson distribution [26]. Therefore, we use the Poisson distribution as the arrival distribution for both attack and non-attack cases.
- We suppose the service rate of each individual IPS follows an exponential distribution, which is common in queueing analysis.

In order to measure the performance of the system, we use *average time in system* of packets as a metric of QoS. We denote T_n (*n* stands for normal) as the acceptable average time in system for packets of benign users in non-attack cases. In general, T_n is a constant. In attack cases, the average time in system varies because the number of attack packets changes. Therefore, we denote it as $T_a(t)$ for a given time point t (*a* stands for attack).

We note that T_n and $T_a(t)$ do not include the time spent in the normal service of the server because this time is the same for both attack and non-attack cases. In other words, the system we study here only includes queue Q and the original IPS or multiple IPSs.

In order to guarantee the QoS of benign users in attack cases, we need to dynamically allocate resources into the battle, and make sure $T_a(t) \leq T_n$ for any time point t.

We use a function $R(\cdot)$ to represent the resource investment. Let variable x be the expected system performance, such as average time in system of requests. Obviously, $R(\cdot)$ depends on x and time point t. We therefore denote it as $R(x,t)$. We also simplify it as $R(x)$ or $R(t)$ if it is clear in the context.

As shown in Fig. 5.1b, we model our mitigation system as an M/M/m queue, namely, one incoming queue with an infinite buffer size, the arrivals following the Poisson distribution, and $m(m \geq 2)$ multiple servers each with an exponential service rate.

With the system model in hand, we can transform our mitigation problem into an optimization problem: minimizing the resource investment $R(t)$ while guaranteeing the QoS for benign users in attack cases. We formulate the problem as follows.

$$mini.R(t)$$

$$s.t. \tag{5.5}$$

$$T_a(t) \leq T_n.$$

5.2.3 Resource Investment Analysis

In order to decide on the investment for a expected quality of service, we have to define an executable investment function $R(x)$ with respect to a system performance expectation x. Variable x could be a vector to represent specific requirements of different resources, such as $x = < CPU, memory, IO, bandwidth >$.

For feasibility reasons, we define $R(x)$ as a linear and non-decreasing function. Let x, y be two different system performance expectations. Then we have the following properties of this investment function.

$$\begin{cases} R(x) & = 0, & x = 0 \quad (a) \\[2mm] R(x) & \leq R(y), & 0 \leq x \leq y \ (b) \\[2mm] R(ax+by) = aR(x) + bR(y), & a, b \in \mathbb{R}. \quad (c) \end{cases} \qquad (5.6)$$

In practice, the current CSPs, such as Amazon EC2, offer resources in terms of instance. An instance includes a fixed amount of various resources, e.g. memory and IO. In other words, an instance is the basic unit for resource allocation. In this case, Eq. (5.6) does reflect this practice very well.

5.2.4 System Analysis for Non-attack Cases

For a web based service in non-attack cases, it is generally accepted that the arrival rate of queue Q follows the Poisson distribution, whose probability density function is defined as

$$P\{X = k\} = \frac{\lambda^k e^{-\lambda}}{k!}, k=0,1,.... \qquad (5.7)$$

For non-attack cases as shown in Fig. 5.1a, the system can be naturally modeled as an M/M/1/∞ queue. We denote the packet arrival rate as λ, and the service rate of the IPS as μ.

People usually derive a parameter called *utility rate* or *busy rate* as the ratio of the arrival rate and the service rate. In this case, we denote it as

$$\rho_n = \frac{\lambda}{\mu}. \qquad (5.8)$$

Usually, we need to make sure $\rho_n < 1$ in order to keep the system in a stable state.

Based on queueing theory [26], we know the probability of the system stays state π_k (namely, there are k packets in the system) is

$$\begin{cases} \pi_0 = 1 - \frac{\lambda}{\mu} \\[3mm] \pi_k = \left(\frac{\lambda}{\mu}\right)^k \pi_0. \end{cases} \qquad (5.9)$$

The probability density of the time in system is

$$P\{T = t\} = (\mu - \lambda)e^{-(\mu - \lambda)t}, \qquad (5.10)$$

for $t > 0$. The average time spent in the IPS system is

$$T_n = \frac{1}{\mu - \lambda} = \frac{1}{(\frac{1}{\rho_n} - 1)\lambda}. \tag{5.11}$$

Naturally, we assume T_n meets users' expectations of service. We will use T_n as a benchmark of QoS for benign users when the cloud hosted server is under a DDoS attack.

5.2.5 System Analysis for Attack Cases

In the case of a cloud customer being subjected to a DDoS attack as shown in Fig. 5.1b, and based on our proposal, the cloud will clone multiple IPSs to counter the attack in order to guarantee the QoS for benign users.

It is natural that we model the mitigation system using the M/M/m model: Poisson arrival rate and multiple (m) servers with an exponential service rate.

For the sake of neatness in the analysis, we make the following definition.

Definition 5.2.1. Attack strength is the total number of arrivals to a victim for a given time interval when a DDoS attack is ongoing.

From this definition, we know an attack strength includes both benign packets and attack packets. For the sake of simplicity, we represent an attack strength as $r(r \geq 1)$ (where r is a real number) times of the arrival rate of non-attack cases. As we denote the arrival rate of non-attack cases as λ, an attack strength is therefore denoted as $r\lambda$. The service rate for each IPS is still μ as it was in the non-attack case, and all IPSs share the workload. Once again, based on queueing theory [26], we have the following system service rate μ_k (k servers in service).

$$\mu_k = min[k\mu, m\mu] = \begin{cases} k\mu & k \leq m \\ \\ m\mu & m \leq k. \end{cases} \tag{5.12}$$

We obtain the $\pi_k (0 \leq k \leq \infty)$ (the probability of k packets in the system) as follows.

$$\pi_k = \begin{cases} \pi_0 \frac{(m\rho)^k}{k!} & k \leq m \\ \\ \pi_0 \frac{\rho^k m^m}{m!} & m \leq k, \end{cases} \tag{5.13}$$

where ρ is the system busy rate, which is defined in a multiple homogeneous server case as

$$\rho = \frac{r\lambda}{m\mu}. \tag{5.14}$$

Similarly, we have to make sure $\rho < 1$ in order to keep the system in a stable state.

In Eq. (5.13), π_0 represents the probability of a state of the system that there are no packets in the queue, including the initial state of the system. π_0 is an important parameter in queueing analysis, and it is defined as follows in the M/M/m model.

$$\pi_0 = \left[1 + \sum_{k=1}^{m-1} \frac{(m\rho)^k}{k!} + \sum_{k=m}^{\infty} \frac{(m\rho)^k}{k!} \frac{1}{m^{k-m}} \right]^{-1}. \tag{5.15}$$

Opposite to state π_0, we have π_{m+}, which is the probability that a packet has to wait when it arrives in the system. π_{m+} is expressed as

$$\pi_{m+} = \sum_{k=m+1}^{\infty} \pi_k$$

$$= \pi_0 \frac{(m\rho)^m}{m!(1-\rho)} \tag{5.16}$$

$$= 1 - \sum_{k=0}^{m} \pi_0 \frac{(m\rho)^k}{k!}. \tag{5.17}$$

From a system viewpoint, we are interested in the average time spent in the system, $\overline{T_a(t)}$. Here, the number of servers, m, is also a factor on $\overline{T_a(t)}$. We therefore express it more explicitly as $\overline{T_a(t,m)}$, which is given as follows.

$$\overline{T_a(t,m)} = E[T_a(t,m)]$$

$$= \frac{1}{r\lambda} \left(m\rho + \rho \frac{(m\rho)^m}{m!} \frac{\pi_0}{(1-\rho)^2} \right). \tag{5.18}$$

Combining Eqs. (5.14) and (5.18), we have

$$\overline{T_a(t,m)} = \frac{1}{\mu} + \frac{1}{r\lambda} \frac{(\frac{r\lambda}{\mu})^m}{m!} \frac{\pi_0}{(1 - \frac{r\lambda}{m\mu})^2}. \tag{5.19}$$

As previously discussed, in order to guarantee the QoS for benign users during a DDoS attack, the condition of Eq. (5.5) has to be satisfied. Therefore,

$$\frac{1}{\mu} + \frac{1}{r\lambda} \frac{(\frac{r\lambda}{\mu})^m}{m!} \frac{\pi_0}{(1 - \frac{r\lambda}{m\mu})^2} \le \frac{1}{\mu - \lambda}. \tag{5.20}$$

For simplicity, let

$$f(r,m) = \frac{\lambda}{\mu} - (\mu - \lambda)\frac{(r\lambda)^{m-1}}{m!\mu^m}\frac{\pi_0}{(1 - \frac{r\lambda}{m\mu})^2}, \tag{5.21}$$

where π_0 is determined by Eq. (5.15).

Combining (5.21) and (5.20), we have the constrain for the optimization as

$$f(r,m) \geq 0. \tag{5.22}$$

Moreover, we note that Eq. (5.22) is under the following constrains

$$\begin{cases} r\frac{\lambda}{\mu} < m & (a) \\ \\ r \; > 1 & (b) \\ \\ m \; = 2,3,\ldots, & (c) \end{cases} \tag{5.23}$$

where condition (a) comes from Eq. (5.14).

If Eq. (5.22) does not hold, then it is time to invest more resources to clone one or more IPSs against the ongoing attack.

Usually, a cloud has sufficient idle or reserved resources, which can be used to counter brute force DDoS attacks. We denote the resource for one IPS as R_{IPS}, and the available reserved resources of a cloud as R_c. The maximum IPSs that we can use is then $\left\lfloor \frac{R_c}{R_{IPS}} \right\rfloor$. In a strict sense, on top of the constrains in Eq. (5.23), we have to have one more constrain as follows.

$$m \leq \left\lfloor \frac{R_c}{R_{IPS}} \right\rfloor + 1. \tag{5.24}$$

5.3   A Cloud Firewall Framework Against DDoS Attacks

As we just discussed in the previous section, clouds need firewall or something similar to protect themselves. However, there are few work have been done in the category from literature.

There are plenty of work have been done in terms of traditional firewall. One topic is the efficiency of firewall with the aim to ensure that the firewall does not become a bottleneck for a given system. Rovniagin and Wool [27] modeled the firewall packet matching problem as a mathematical point location problem, and proposed a Geometric Efficient Matching (GEM) algorithm. Their experiments indicated that the proposed algorithm is more space efficient for rule based firewalls. Hu et al. [28] considered the quality of policy of firewall configuration, and

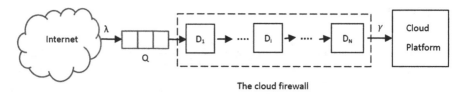

The cloud firewall

Fig. 5.2 The framework of the dynamical firewall for cloud platforms

presented a firewall policy anomaly management framework, which employed a rule based segmentation technique to identify policy anomalies and derive effective anomaly resolutions. Salah et al. [29] proposed a embedded Markov chain based mathematical model for rule-based firewall performance analysis, especially against DDoS attacks. They presented closed form expressions of a number of important performance metrics, such as mean throughput, service time, CPU utilization. As majority of the similar work, they assumed the arrival rate following the Poisson distribution and the service times are independent and exponentially distributed.

In our previous work [30], we proposed a framework of cloud firewall. As shown in Fig. 5.2, the proposed cloud firewall is between the Internet and a cloud platform. All incoming requests will be examined by detectors in a sequence until a detector reports positive. Further actions will be taken, e.g. dropping or blocking related requests.

In general, assume we have N different detectors $D_i(i = 1, 2, \ldots, N)$, each of them aims at one specific anomaly, such as viruses, different DDoS attacks, and information phishing. The packet arrival rate is λ, and the throughput rate is represented by γ.

It is generally accepted that request arrival follows the Poisson distribution.

For each detector $D_i(i = 1, 2, \ldots, N)$, we denote its service rate as μ_i^0. We can easily obtain the average service time of the N detectors as

$$E[\mu^0] = \frac{1}{N} \sum_{j=1}^{N} \mu_j^0. \tag{5.25}$$

In the case that we have no knowledge of the anomaly distribution, we suppose the N detectors share the same probability of positive detection, p $(p > 0)$, then we know the positive detection follows the geometric distribution. Let random variable X be the number of trials, then the probability that we obtain the first positive detection at $k(k \in \mathbb{N})$ is expressed as follows.

$$Pr\{X = k\} = p_k = (1 - p)^{k-1} p. \tag{5.26}$$

The probability cumulative distribution function is

$$F[X \leq k] = 1 - (1 - p)^k. \tag{5.27}$$

The mean of the geometric distribution is

$$E[X] = \frac{1}{p}.\tag{5.28}$$

From a system point of view, we care about the average of system service time, which is

$$\mu = \sum_{k=1}^{N} \left(p_k \cdot \sum_{j=1}^{k} \mu_j^0 \right).\tag{5.29}$$

Based on the Wild theorem, we can rewrite Eq. (5.29) based on Eqs. (5.25) and (5.28).

$$\mu = E[X]E[\mu^0].\tag{5.30}$$

In order to find closed form solutions for our studied objects, we further suppose the service time of N detectors is i.i.d, and follows exponential distribution. This approximation is practical and commonly used in performance evaluation. Let μ_e be the mean of the service time of the detectors, then Eq. (5.30) can be further expressed as

$$\mu = \frac{1}{p}\mu_e.\tag{5.31}$$

As a result, we can model the cloud firewall as a M/M/1 queue with arrival rate λ and service rate μ. Taking advantage of the conclusions of queueing theory [26], we can extract the key performance metrics that we are interested.

First of all, the probability of the system stays state q_k (namely, there are k requests in the system) is

$$\begin{cases} p_0 = 1 - \frac{\lambda}{\mu} \quad = 1 - \frac{p\lambda}{\mu_e}, \\ \\ p_k = \left(\frac{\lambda}{\mu}\right)^k p_0 = \left(\frac{p\lambda}{\mu_e}\right)^k 1 - \frac{p\lambda}{\mu_e}. \end{cases}\tag{5.32}$$

The probability density of the time in system is

$$Pr\{T = t\} = (\mu - \lambda)e^{-(\mu-\lambda)t},\tag{5.33}$$

for $t > 0$.

The average time spent in the firewall system is

$$T = \frac{p}{\mu_e - p\lambda}.\tag{5.34}$$

Based on Eq. (5.34), we obtain the average system throughput

$$\gamma = \frac{1}{T} = \frac{1}{p}\mu_e - \lambda. \tag{5.35}$$

The average number of requests in the system

$$\overline{K} = \sum_{j=1}^{K} k p_k. \tag{5.36}$$

In terms of firewall, we are interested in CPU utilization, which is also referred as to *carried load*. We denote this metric as U_{cpu}, and it can be calculated as

$$U_{cpu} = \gamma\mu = \frac{1}{p}\gamma\mu_e. \tag{5.37}$$

Let ρ be the busy rate of the studied system. From a system viewpoint, in order to make the system stable, the following has to be met.

$$\rho = \frac{p\lambda}{\mu_e} < 1. \tag{5.38}$$

5.3.1   Dynamic Resource Allocation for Cloud Firewall

In this subsection, we focus on how to economically and dynamically allocate resource to meet the requirement of a cloud firewall.

Following the resource investment function Eq. (5.6), in the cloud firewall case, our system requirement x is the average time in system of requests, T, which is defined in Eq. (5.34). In order to avoid our cloud firewall becoming a bottleneck, the time in system for a request has to be limited. Let ΔT be an acceptable threshold for T, then our resource investment problem becomes an optimization issue as follows.

$$\begin{aligned} &minimizeR(T)\\ &s.t.\\ &T \leq \Delta T. \end{aligned} \tag{5.39}$$

5.3.2   Single Chain vs Multiple Parallel Chains

Suppose a single detection chain with a given resource works well for an arrival rate λ. As the number of requests to a cloud platform is dynamic. Let $m \in \mathbb{R}$ and $m > 1$ be the *traffic strength*. Intuitively, when the arrival rate increase to $m\lambda$, we should

Fig. 5.3 The two options for
resource investment for cloud
firewall

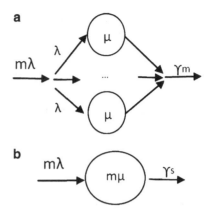

invest more resource to handle the traffic. One problem rises naturally, when the
number of requests increases, how should we invest our resource?

In general, there are two options to deal with this case: (1) clone $\lceil m-1 \rceil$ parallel
detection chains based on the original detection chain; (2) keep the original detection
chain, but increase the service capability of each detector to $m\mu$. We show these two
options in Fig. 5.3. We are interested about which one is a better investment.

In order to conduct the comparison, we use service rate as a study object in $R()$.
When the arrival rate increase to $m\lambda$. The resource that we need for the multiple
detection chain strategy is $R(m\mu)$. Let x be the expected service rate of the single
detection chain strategy, then,

$$\frac{1}{x-m\lambda} = \Delta T = \frac{1}{\mu - \lambda}. \tag{5.40}$$

It is easy to find that

$$x = \mu + (m-1)\lambda. \tag{5.41}$$

As $\lambda < \mu$, combining this with Eq. (5.41), we have

$$x < m\mu. \tag{5.42}$$

Based on the property (b) of investment function (5.6), we have

$$R(x) < R(m\mu). \tag{5.43}$$

Namely, for a given performance metric, the resource needed by the single detection
chain is less than that by the multiple detection chain strategy.

Furthermore, we expect to know for the same resource investment, how much
gain we can obtain from a single detection chain strategy compared with the multiple
detection chain strategy. We denote the system throughput for the two strategies as
γ_m (multiple detection chains) and γ_s (single detection chain), respectively, and their
average time in system for a request as T_m and T_s, respectively.

As shown in Fig. 5.3a, the average time in system for the multiple detection chain is equivalent to one of its parallel detection chain. Based on Eq. (5.34), we have

$$T_m = \frac{1}{\mu - \lambda}. \tag{5.44}$$

At the same time, based on Fig. 5.3b, we obtain the average time in system for a single detection chain as

$$T_s = \frac{1}{m\mu - m\lambda} = \frac{1}{m}T_m. \tag{5.45}$$

Therefore, we obtain

$$\gamma_s = m\gamma_m. \tag{5.46}$$

As we know $m > 1$, therefore, for the same resource investment, the single detection chain strategy outperforms the multiple detection chain strategy m times.

References

1. M. Armbrust, A. Fox, R. Griffith, A. D. Joseph, R. H. Katz, A. Konwinski, G. Lee, D. A. Patterson, A. Rabkin, I. Stoica, and M. Zaharia, "Above the clouds: A berkeley view of cloud computing," EECS Department, University of California, Berkeley, Tech. Rep. UCB/EECS-2009-28, Feb 2009.
2. C. Peng, M. Kim, Z. Zhang, and H. Lei, "Vdn: Virtual machine image distribution network for cloud data centers," in Proceedings of the INFOCOM, 2012, pp. 181–189.
3. S. Subashini and V. Kavitha, "A survey on security issues in service delivery models of cloud computing," Journal of Network and Computer Applications, vol. 34, no. 1, pp. 1–11, 2011.
4. R. Bhadauria, R. Chaki, N. Chaki, and S. Sanyal, "A survey on security issues in cloud computing," CoRR, vol. abs/1109.5388, 2011.
5. Z. Duan, X. Yuan, and J. Chandrashekar, "Controlling ip spoofing through interdomain packet filters," IEEE Transactions on Dependable and Secure Computing, vol. 5, no. 1, pp. 22–36, 2008.
6. H. Wang, C. Jin, and K. G. Shin, "Defense against spoofed ip traffic using hop-count filtering," IEEE/ACM Transactions on Networking, vol. 15, no. 1, pp. 40–53, 2007.
7. Y. Kim, W. C. Lau, M. C. Chuah, and H. J. Chao, "Packetscore: A statistics-based packet filtering scheme against distributed denial-of-service attacks," IEEE Transactions on Dependable and Secure Computing, vol. 3, no. 2, pp. 141–155, 2006.
8. S. Yu, W. Zhou, W. Jia, S. Guo, Y. Xiang, and F. Tang, "Discriminating ddos attacks from flash crowds using flow correlation coefficient," IEEE Transactions on Parallel Distributed Systems, vol. 23, no. 6, pp. 794–805, 2012.
9. S. Yu, S. Guo, and I. Stojmenovic, "Can we beat legitimate cyber behavior mimicking attacks from botnets?" in Proceedings of the INFOCOM, 2012.
10. D. K. Y. Yau, J. C. S. Lui, F. Liang, and Y. Yam, "Defending against distributed denial-of-service attacks with max-min fair server-centric router throttles," IEEE/ACM Transactions on Networking, vol. 13, no. 1, pp. 29–42, 2005.

11. R. Chen, J.-M. Park, and R. Marchany, "A divide-and-conquer strategy for thwarting distributed denial-of-service attacks," *IEEE Transactions on Parallel and Distributed Systems*, vol. 18, no. 5, pp. 577–588, 2007.

12. Y. Chen, K. Hwang, and W.-S. Ku, "Collaborative detection of ddos attacks over multiple network domains," *IEEE Transactions on Parallel and Distributed Systems*, vol. 18, no. 12, pp. 1649–1662, 2007.

13. J. Francois, I. Aib, and R. Boutaba, "Firecol, a collaborative protection network for the detection of flooding ddos attacks," *IEEE/ACM Transactions on Networking*, vol. 20, no. 6, pp. 1828–1841, 2012.

14. M. H. Sqalli, F. Al-Haidari, and K. Salah, "Edos-shield - a two-steps mitigation technique against edos attacks in cloud computing," in *Proceedings of the UCC*, 2011, pp. 49–56.

15. J. Idziorek, M. Tannian, and D. Jacobson, "The insecurity of cloud utility models," *IT Professional*, vol. 15, no. 2, pp. 22–27, 2013.

16. A. El-Atawy, E. Al-Shaer, T. Tran, and R. Boutaba, "Adaptive early packet filtering for protecting firewalls against dos attacks," in *Proceedings of the INFOCOM*, 2009.

17. R. Lua and K. C. Yow, "Mitigating ddos attacks with transparent and intelligent fast-flux swarm network," *IEEE Network*, no. July/August, pp. 28–33, 2011.

18. J. Chen, Y. Wang, and X. Wang, "On-demand security architecture for cloud computing," *Computer*, vol. 99, no. PrePrints, 2012.

19. CloudWatch, http://aws.amazon.com/cloudwatch/.

20. http://aws.amazon.com/ec2/pricing/.

21. R. Wartel, T. Cass, B. Moreira, E. Roche, M. Guijarro, S. Goasguen, and U. Schwickerath, "Image distribution mechanisms in large scale cloud providers," in *Proceedings of the CloudCom*, 2010, pp. 112–117.

22. J. Zhu, Z. Jiang, and Z. Xiao, "Twinkle: A fast resource provisioning mechanism for internet services," in *Proceedings of the INFOCOM*, 2011, pp. 802–810.

23. S. Yu, Y. Tian, S. Guo, and D. O. Wu, "Can we beat ddos attacks in clouds," *IEEE Transactions on Parallel Distributed Systems*, vol. accepted, 2013.

24. H. Khazaei, J. V. Misic, and V. B. Misic, "Performance analysis of cloud computing centers using m/g/m/m+r queuing systems," *IEEE Transactions on Parallel and Distributed Systems*, vol. 23, no. 5, pp. 936–943, 2012.

25. J. F. C. Kingman, "The first erlang century - and the next," *Queueing Systems*, vol. 63, no. 1–4, pp. 3–12, 2009.

26. L. Kleinrock, *Queueing Systems*. Wiley Interscience, 1975, vol. I: Theory.

27. D. Rovniagin and A. Wool, "The geometric efficient matching algorithm for firewalls," *IEEE Transactions on Dependable and Secure Computing*, vol. 8, no. 1, pp. 147–159, 2011.

28. H. Hu, G.-J. Ahn, and K. Kulkarni, "Detecting and resolving firewall policy anomalies," *IEEE Transactions on Dependable and Secure Computing*, vol. 9, no. 3, pp. 318–331, 2012.

29. K. Salah, K. Elbadawi, and R. Boutaba, "Performance modeling and analysis of network firewalls," *IEEE Transactions on Network and Service Management*, vol. 9, no. 1, pp. 12–21, 2012.

30. S. Yu, W. Zhou, R. Doss, and S. Guo, "A general cloud firewall framework with dynamic resource allocation," in *Proceedings of the IEEE ICC*, 2013.

Chapter 6
Future Work

Abstract We summarize the book and discuss the possible future work.

In this book brief, we have gone through the research work on DDoS attack and defence to date. We have discussed the short history of DoS and DDoS attacks, the reasons why it is hard to handle or eliminate such attacks, DDoS attack detection, attack source traceback, and DDoS attack and defence in cloud environment.

Denial of service attack is an open problem today, we believe it will be a critical threat in cyberspace for a long time. Usually, information security is classified into three categories: confidentiality, integrity, and availability. We can see clearly that DDoS attack falls in the availability category. Obviously, Denial of service is a big topic in information security. Due to its nature, DDoS attack and defence is an endless battle between attackers and defenders. Once defenders design a new defence method or eliminate a vulnerability, attackers will invent new strategies or methods to circumvent them to achieve their malicious goals, and vice visa.

Information and communication technology sector is a fast developing part of the whole world. New hardware, new computing models, and new platforms are continuously invented, developed and used in human society. We are witnessing the emerging of many new ideas and applications in the cyberspace, such as Cloud Computing [1], Big Data [2], Energy-harvesting Networks [3], and so on. It is hard for designers to predict the possible vulnerabilities of their new products. As a result, defenders are generally passive in the battle against attackers. In addition, these new products will introduce new security and privacy problems and may threat to some existing solutions. For example, the cheap and available super computing power from cloud causes a great threat to the time complexity based encryption mechanism.

We have to note that DDoS related research is only a very small part of cyber security. In order to address cyber security problems, we have to obtain a better and deeper understanding of the cyberspace. As indicated by the American Research Council, the research on *network science* just recently started [4]. Moreover, as the

S. Yu, *Distributed Denial of Service Attack and Defense*, SpringerBriefs in Computer Science, DOI 10.1007/978-1-4614-9491-1_6, © The Author(s) 2014

Web and the Internet are getting more and more huge and complex, we face many challenges to understand these giant networks.

One essential problem that we facing is that we do not have a feasible fundamental theory for networks. It is commonly accepted by the networking community that we lack theories for networks. Although there are many different theoretical tools that serve specific problems well, however, they are usually effective in a narrow range, rather than a wide circumstance. The main tools for networking are Graph Theory and Queueing Theory. There have been some developments in the two categories for computer science, such as the random graph model [5] in Graph Theory, and network calculus [6,7] and stochastic network calculus [8] in Queueing Theory. However, all the developments are far from the final goal. This is similar to the blind men and the elephant issue, and we need a global view of the problem. We have seen some effort in narrowing the gap between theories and applications in the domain of computer science, such as the effort at the end of last century [9], and a recent work [10]. However, we do not see a ground-breaking progress in this direction.

If we quickly cast our eyes to the history of science, we find that the necessary mathematical tools were always in place far before people actually used them for ground-breaking work. For example, Differential Geometry was quite mature when Albert Einstein used it for his work. Today, mathematics has far advanced in each of its branches, e.g., the recent development in number theory [11]. As a result, we should be confident that the mathematical tools are already available for us to model the Web, the Internet, and other complex networks. Our job is to deeply understand these mathematical tools and fit them into our computer science problems. If necessary, we may invent new mathematical tools to solve our problems.

In terms of information technology, human beings had the first radio tube in 1904, and the first television in 1924. However, it was 1949 when Claude Shannon discovered Information Theory, which is a fundamental theory for information technology. We know the APARNET was implemented in the late 1960s, and became a public network as the Internet in the 1990s. So far, we do not have a commonly accepted theory for the giant network. However, it is not difficult to believe that the expected theory will be in place sooner or later.

It is time to dig harder, folks.

References

1. M. Armbrust, A. Fox, R. Griffith, A. D. Joseph, R. H. Katz, A. Konwinski, G. Lee, D. A. Patterson, A. Rabkin, I. Stoica, and M. Zaharia, "Above the clouds: A berkeley view of cloud computing," EECS Department, University of California, Berkeley, Tech. Rep. UCB/EECS-2009-28, Feb 2009.
2. X. Wu, X. Zhu, C.-Q. Wu, and W. Ding, "Data mining with big data," *IEEE Transactions on Knowledge and Data Engineering*, in press.
3. L. Huang and M. Neely, "Utility optimal scheduling in energy-havesting networks," *IEEE/ACM Transactions on Networking*, in press.

4. http://www.nap.edu/catalog/11516.html.

5. P. Erdos and A. Renyi, "On random graphs. i," *Publicationes Mathematicae*, vol. 6, pp. 290–297, 1959.

6. R. L. Cruz, "A calculus for network delay, part i: Network elements in isolation," *IEEE Transactions on Information Theory*, vol. 37, no. 1, pp. 114–131, 1991.

7. ——, "A calculus for network delay, part ii: Network analysis," *IEEE Transactions on Information Theory*, vol. 37, no. 1, pp. 132–141, 1991.

8. Y. Jiang, "Analysis of stochastic service guarantees in communication networks: A basic calculus," *CoRR*, vol. abs/cs/0511008, 2005.

9. A. Ephremides and B. E. Hajek, "Information theory and communication networks: An unconsummated union," *IEEE Transactions on Information Theory*, vol. 44, no. 6, pp. 2416–2434, 1998.

10. A. Goldsmith, M. Effros, R. Koetter, M. Médard, A. E. Ozdaglar, and L. Zheng, "Beyond shannon: the quest for fundamental performance limits of wireless ad hoc networks," *IEEE Communications Magazine*, vol. 49, no. 5, pp. 195–205, 2011.

11. Y. Zhang, "Bounded gaps between primes," *Annual of Mathematics*, in press.